To Charles,
Wishing you a very happy
Birthday, 82 love. Peggy.

OLD EXETER

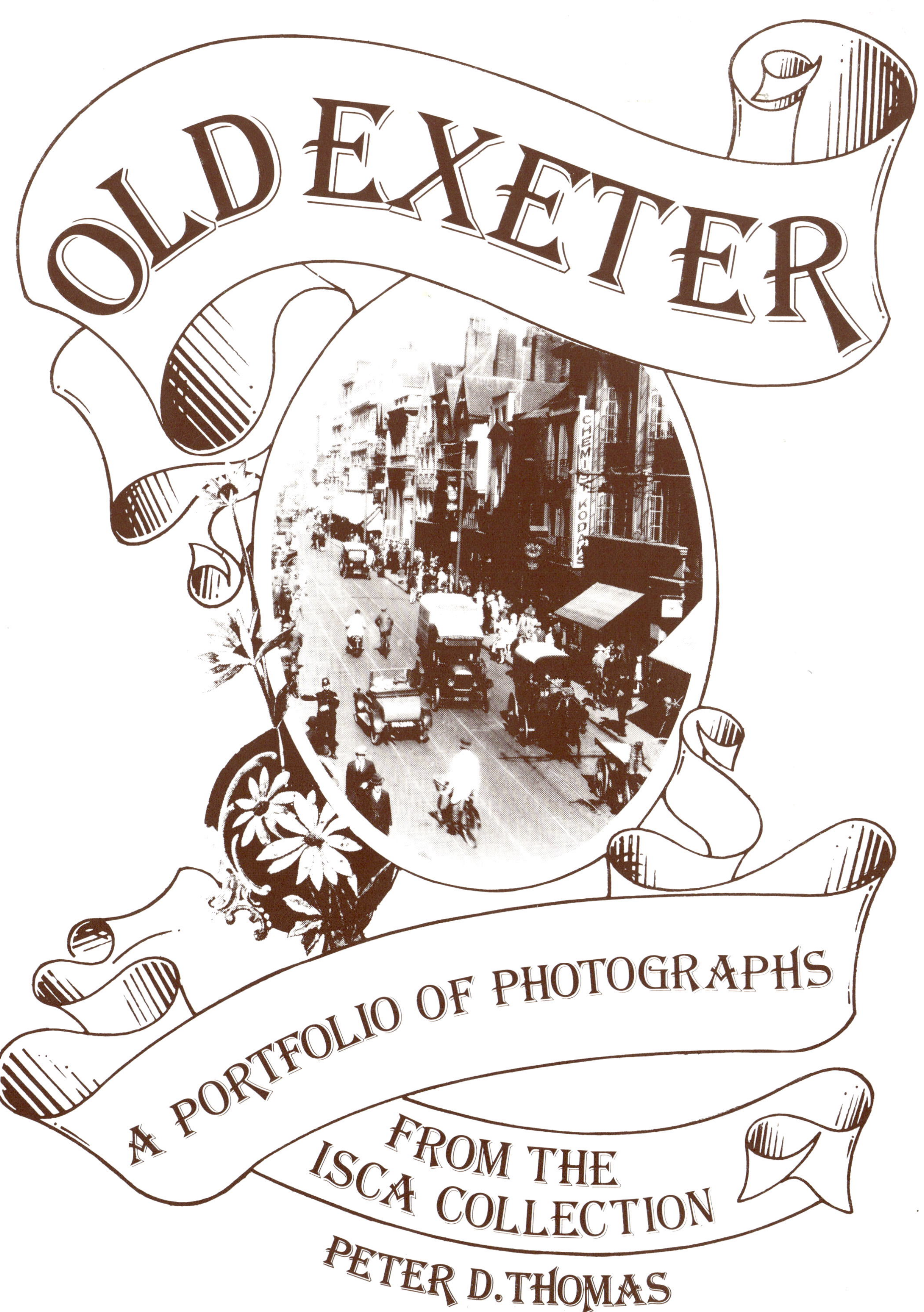

Webb & Bower
EXETER, ENGLAND

First published in Great Britain 1977
by Baron Jay Limited
Reprinted 1979

This edition with new printed case and endpapers
published in Great Britain 1981 by
Webb & Bower (Publishers) Limited
9 Colleton Crescent, Exeter, Devon EX2 4BY

British Library Cataloguing in Publication Data

Old Exeter.—2nd ed.
1. Exeter (Devon)—History—Pictorial works
2. Exeter (Devon)—Description—Views
I. Thomas, Peter D.
942.3'56'0810222 DA690.E9

ISBN 0-906671-66-3

Printed by P.D.S. Printers, Plymouth, Devon

Bound by Butler and Tanner Limited
Frome, Somerset

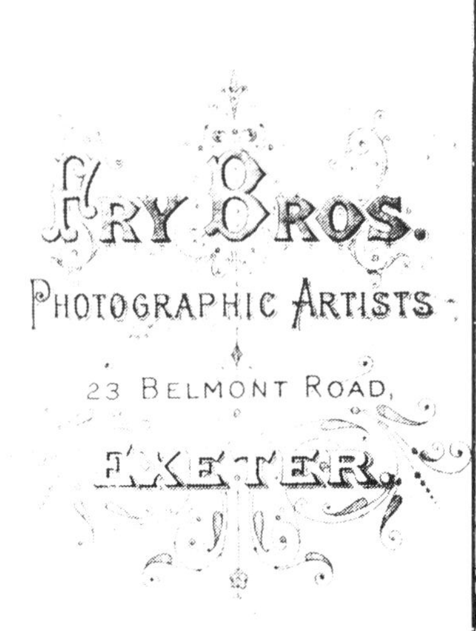

THE ISCA COLLECTION

Started about four years ago by Peter Thomas, the ISCA COLLECTION contains a wealth of visual information on pre-war Exeter. Much to the amazement of the author the city of Exeter seemed to lack any quantity of photographs showing the city as it used to be. By chance, an extensive collection of negatives was purchased from a local studio that was closing down. It comprised some 40,000 negatives.

Perusal revealed much of OLD EXETER in its hey-day and many places that had long since disappeared.

Using this as a base, the collection has been extended over the years and now is probably the most extensive record library of OLD EXETER. A number of exhibitions have been arranged at the City Library, the Museum and the University.

The ISCA COLLECTION is now recorded by the Royal Photographic Society in the British Photographic Record, a directory of historical photographic collections.

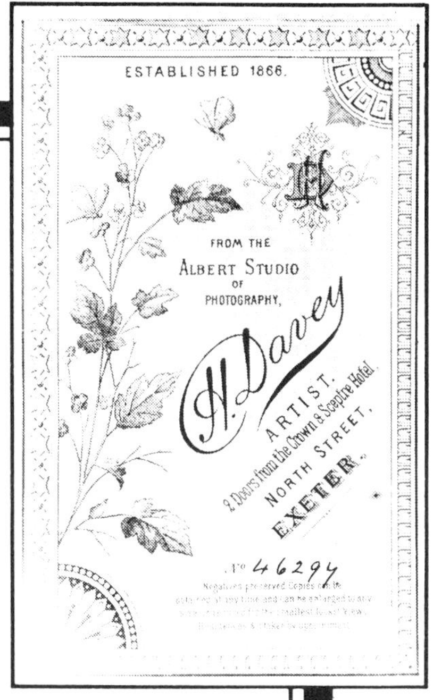

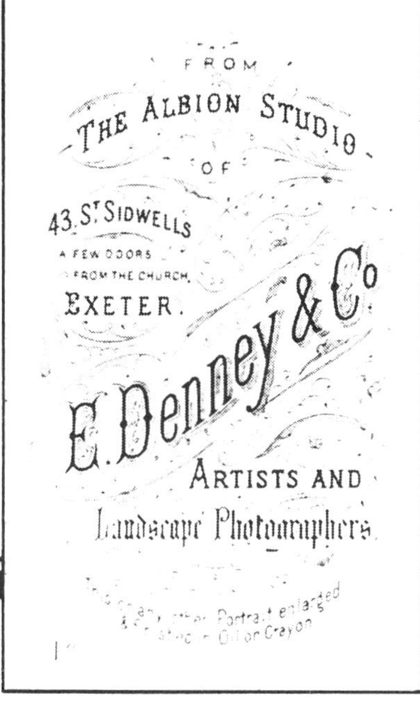

ACKNOWLEDGEMENTS

For supplying material and information on the background of OLD EXETER my grateful thanks to, Mr. M. Alford, Mr. F. Baxter, Mr. Flay, Dr. R. K. Fortesque Foulkes, Mrs. Holland, Mr. M. Milton, Mr. C. Sercombe. My appreciation to Mr. G. Everett. A special thank you to Miss M. Hockmuth for her great kindness and help. The Royal Albert Memorial Museum: Exeter City Library (especially Mr. G. Paley). Sincere thanks to my friend and colleague Mr. S. Salter for his enthusiasm, without which it would have been much more difficult to piece OLD EXETER together. To Mr. P. Jones for his patience and help with my efforts.

Lastly, my thanks to my family who have put up with my litter all over the house. To my brother Clive, my everlasting gratitude for all his interest and help, without whose advice and aid many things would not have been possible.

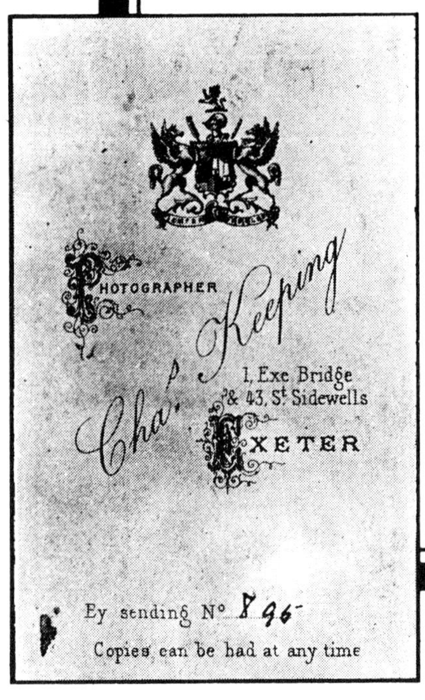

To my parents with great affection

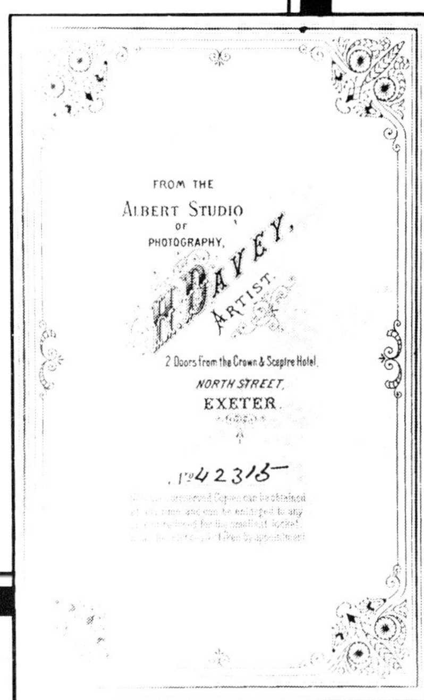

PETER DAVID THOMAS

Born February 1948 in Exeter
Resident of Exeter
Secondary Modern School education (Episcopal School)

Left school and spent 5 years in the building trade doing quantity surveying and general office duties. Left at 20 and joined a photographic retail business. A keen interest in photography from an early age due to encouragement and help from a close family friend. All later photographic knowledge self taught and eventually he acquired a large collection of photographic equipment connected with the history of photography. The collection called the "Isca Collection" has also acquired the largest quantity of prewar Exeter photographs that exists (to the knowledge of the Author). Exhibitions have been staged and lectures given on the history of photography and "Old Exeter". Photographs have been sent to Her Majesty Queen Elizabeth The Queen Mother, Sir Peter Scott, and Lord Clinton.

The Collection has been recorded by the Royal Photographic Society in the historical section.

Peter Thomas has travelled in many European countries and has a keen interest in travelling and meeting foreign people.

An ardent supporter of the World Wildlife Fund, he is Chairman of a regional fund raising group for the fund in Exeter. In December 1976 he departed for a 6 month trip to Mexico and Australia. The intention being to photograph the wildlife of both countries and make the material available to The World Wildlife Fund for educational projects. Some 10,000 slides and over 5,000 black and white photos are hoped for.

It is hoped in the future that further publications may emerge from The Isca Collection.

FOREWORD

I am very pleased to have the opportunity to write a foreword to this very interesting collection of photographs of Exeter.

In its excellent presentation a very graphic history of the City is shown. Details are brought to life and for many a new insight into the buildings are shown in greater detail.

The photographs and the way in which they have been presented and arranged brings to life the events and occasions in the City's history. People and their way of life have been brought into focus in a way which allows the reader to live over the times and activities of people, giving a very human touch to this book.

Peter Thomas has with his photographic sense been able to present in this book a very varied and worthwhile collection of photographs which he has in his possession, and with his expertise has been able to show off the photographic art, produced by a variety of photographers, to its best advantage.

Rt. Hon. Lord Clinton,
Heanton Satchville

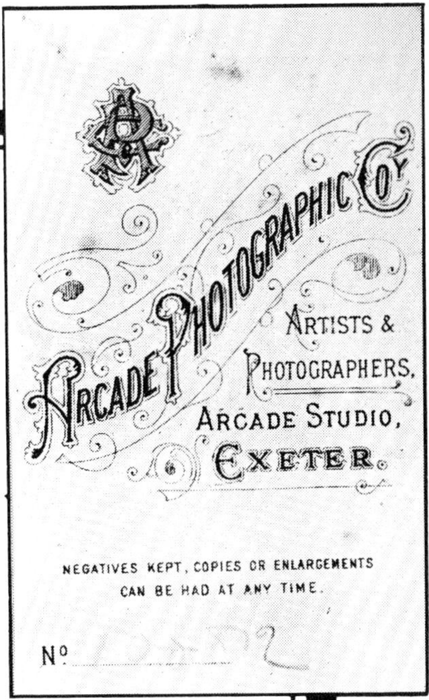
Arcade Photographic Coy
Artists & Photographers,
Arcade Studio,
Exeter.
Negatives kept, copies or enlargements can be had at any time.
No.

CONTENTS

Artist & Photographer
C. Keeping
1 Exe Bridge
Exeter
Copies of this portrait can always be had by sending No.

INTRODUCTION

I am proud to present the first book of its kind to be produced on The City of Exeter, County seat of Devon. I hope that it will give an insight to those who did not know Exeter before the war and a sentimental reminder for those who knew it as it then was. It is difficult when one looks at Exeter today to imagine how it used to be, but I hope that as you turn the pages of this book it will bring to you the atmosphere of the old City. It is not intended that this should be a written historical document. What has been strived for is that it should be a highly illustrated book of good photographic quality, which will convey to you the intimacy of its streets, its characters and life. For centuries Exeter has been an historical City and there are many happenings which have been recorded, but I can only show what has been recorded since the age of the camera. So my visual record of Exeter should start around 1860 to 1870. We shall be lucky to find any existing records before this date, as photography did not come into general use until 1888. Records have relied on those who have recorded not only Exeter's streets and buildings, but people, social events and occasions. My original source has come mainly from the collection of the late Henry Wykes, who was a professional photographer in Exeter around 1912. Fortunately, Mr. Wykes faithfully recorded many of the streets and other subjects in Exeter. From his basic work I have expanded this collection to include numerous other items and views, to give as wide a panorama of the Exeter scene as possible.

It is tragic to consider what was lost of OLD EXETER during the war and how Exeter's character has changed and is still changing. The quaint streets and little courtyards that existed in profusion have virtually disappeared. Today, one is confronted with wide streets and an architecture that utilises straight unsympathetic lines. Gracious curves, uneven roofs, old timbers and cobbled streets that existed for centuries, were suddenly to disappear within four hours, under the heavy bombardment of Hitler's incendiary and high explosive bombs.

The City that was called the "Jewel of the West" was torn from its golden setting and smashed. When the burning stopped and dust settled, to the horror of surviving Exeter residents much of their City lay in ruins. Those who were born at the end of the war and after, can perhaps remember playing in some of the ruins.

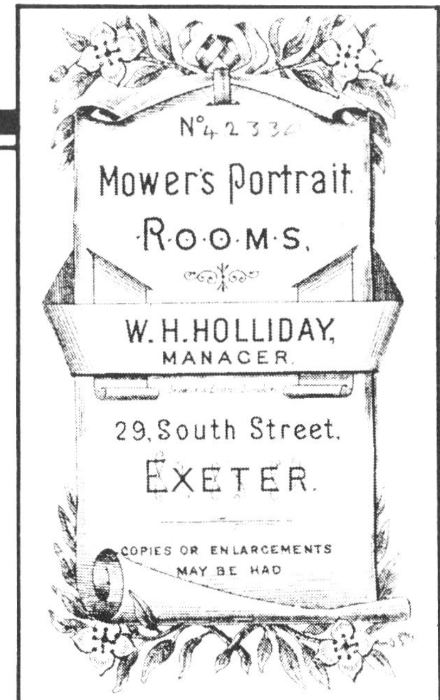

The old Lower Market for instance and the bombed sites of South Street; or perhaps in the lower half of Paris Street; Coombe Street and the corner of High Street and Longbrook Street. I wonder if any of those children ever thought what was originally on these sites?

The memory is not always reliable and I wonder if you have been asked "what place stood there?" After a few minutes thought, you say:- "Oh yes that was such and such a place; No it was that shop – or was it?" It is surprising, but in a short time one can forget places that one used to see every day. Thus the camera has come to our aid and faithfully records what is before it. Not only does it record the scene for us, but also can give us visually some new realisations. How many times do you observe what is perhaps only a short distance above your head? The photograph reduces scale and one can scan the scene at leisure. The shapes of the buildings and their structures and many minor details we may not notice in a casual glance.

The choice of photographs to use is difficult so this first look at OLD EXETER is aesthetic.

Back to the days of dodging the horses and carts, trams running up and down Fore Street, joining the celebrations for the opening of the new Exe Bridge, a drink in the Globe Hotel, Cathedral Yard, and what about a whirl in Dellers Cafe to the Palm Court Orchestra.

I am sure that the appearance of such photographs will evoke many memories for people who knew OLD EXETER and I think for many younger people OLD EXETER is going to be quite a surprise. Therefore, can I say that it is not good enough just to look at this book from the point of view merely of memory, but also to look critically, because the present City of Exeter is an excellent example of what can happen to your environment. Indeed, our City boasted a host of historical buildings many absolutely unique and beautiful. It was not only the war that destroyed a very fine old City, but Councils, Planners and a host of others who have sought change in the name of "progress" as they prefer it to be called. Certainly one can feel great sadness at the loss of so much, but it also makes one more determined to fight to preserve what cannot possibly be replaced.

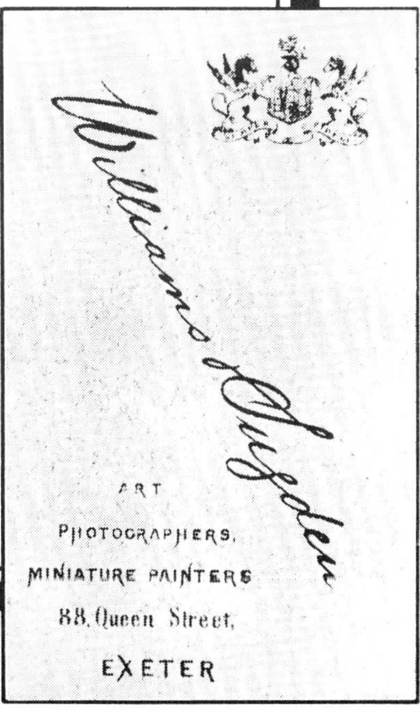

THE ISCA COLLECTION

OLD EXETER

ie Old City viewed from the air. Probably one of the earliest aerial views of Exeter taken around 1927. Clearly the High Street is picted like a main artery of the city. The Cathedral stands ever dominant, behind Bedford Circus built on the site of an ancient ominican Monastry. An important part of the City omitted from the picture is the river Exe from which Exeter takes its name. ie Road would continue from High Street to Fore Street and then to the River below the bottom of the picture. It is interesting note how tightly packed the buildings and houses were, in those pre war days.

A view of the Old Stone Exe Bridge, looking up Fore Street. You can also see the studio of Charles Keeping, photographer, just left of the bridge.

THE EXE BRIDGE

Exeter owes it's location and importance to the fact that it was situated on the last suitable place for crossing the river Exe at its seaward end. Until 1231 the only means of crossing the river was by ferry boat or a very narrow wooden bridge. This would only take the weight of a human being. There was also a ford, but people frequently lost their lives trying to get into the City.

The first proper bridge of stone with twelve magnificent arches was built thanks to Walter Gervaise, Mayor of Exeter. The foundations were laid in 1257. Through the passage of time it was repaired and improved, but eventually traffic was too heavy and a new bridge was built in 1770. A three arched bridge this time as seen in our next photograph. The cost of building was £30,000. At first there were problems with construction, but after the foundations were laid on solid rock no more problems arose. It is interesting to note the first vehicle to cross the new bridge was a hearse!

With the coming of the tram it was again necessary to replace the old bridge with a new structure. Made in iron, a single span bridge was opened in 1905 by the Mayor C. Perry. To maintain access a wooden pontoon bridge was situated beside it and dismantled after the construction was completed. Alas, the bridge has now disappeared and been replaced by a concrete structure. A bonus derived from this and the revised schemes is the discovery and exposure of the remains of the old medieval stone bridge.

It is most fortunate that we have some excellent records of the old stone bridge, the new iron bridge, its construction and the opening ceremony. These have been reproduced from some fine 12 x 10 glass plates that are still in existence.

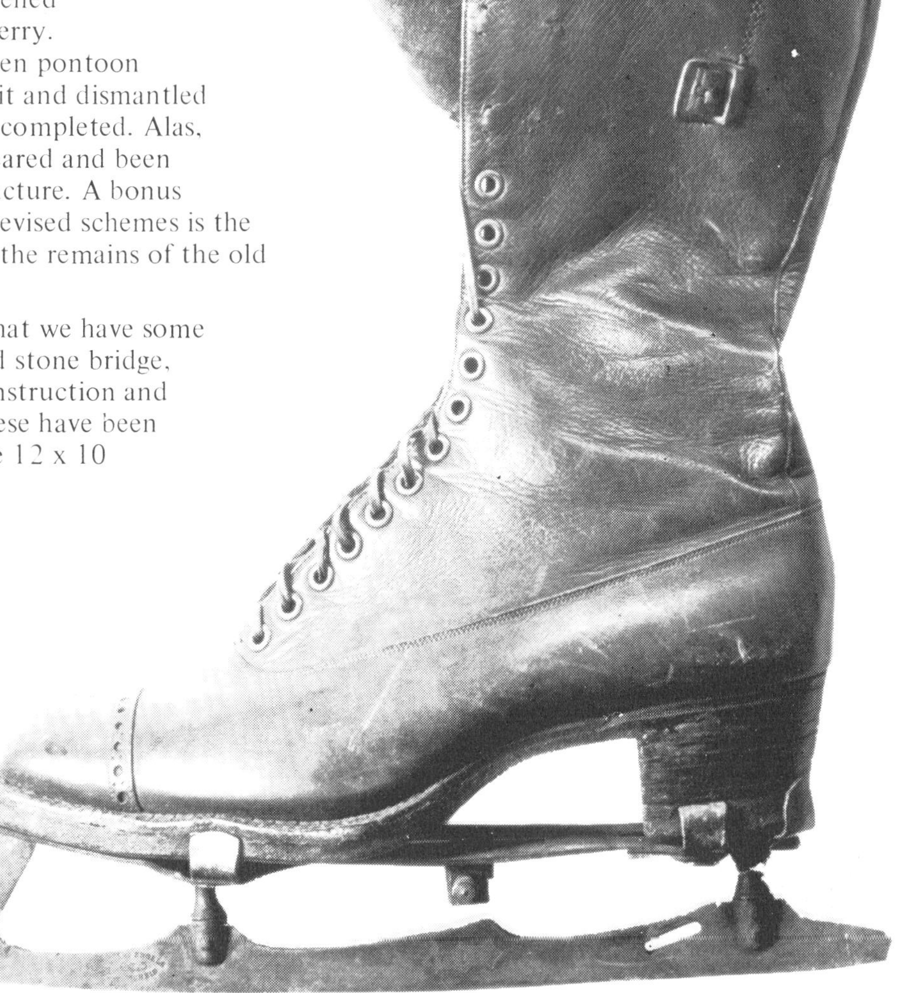

The frozen river Exe under the Old Stone Bridge. *(circa 1890)*

Having fun with a makeshift Ice Yacht on the frozen Exe

The single span Iron Bridge during construction. Note the use of barges to help with this mammoth task.

Putting the finishing touches to the New Exe Bridge in 1905, while work on dismantling the wood pontoon bridge used during it's construction goes ahead.

The official opening of the New Exe Bridge by Major C. Perry in 1905. A great occasion, as it brought the era of the tram to Exeter.

Another view of the grand opening of the New Exe Bridge on 29th March 1905.

The completed bridge ready for use by the new trams.

The New Bridge weighed 430 tons and the ornamental work and parapet – made in cast iron – add a further 110 tons. The road over the Old Bridge was 25 feet wide, while that over the New Bridge was 36 feet wide, with an 8 feet path, 3 feet wider than the old. The total cost of the new structure and the temporary wooden bridge was £25,000.

The Old Stone Bridge over the Exe, which was demolished in 1903 to make way for the new single span Iron Bridge.

(a)

(b)

(c)

How Exonians obtained their water supplies, no mod. cons in those days.

(a) The pump at the mint.
(b) Old Shillhay Bridge.
(c) Dipping Steps under the Battery.
(d) The buckets and hoops of the water carriers.
(e) The ancient city water works.

(d)

(e)

ESTABLISHED UPWARDS OF 60 YEARS.

RICHARD ROUSE,

PLUMBER,

Beer Engine Manufacturer,

GAS FITTER, &c.,

74, ST. SIDWELL'S STREET,

EXETER.

HYDRAULIC PUMPS AND WATER CLOSETS
Fixed on the most approved principles.

MILLINERY, MANTLE, AND BONNET
SHOW ROOMS,
53, HIGH STREET, 53,
EXETER.

MRS. CHARLES ADAMS

Solicits an inspection of her SHOW ROOMS, which are now replete with all the Latest Novelties.

Mourning Orders

EXECUTED ON THE SHORTEST NOTICE.

MUSLIN AND LACE GOODS
IN GREAT VARIETY.

WEDDING ORDERS CAREFULLY ATTENDED TO.

THE ATHENÆUM PIANOFORTE & GENERAL MUSIC
WAREHOUSE,

20, BEDFORD CIRCUS,
EXETER.
(Removed from 234, High Street.)

PIANOFORTES,
HARMONIUMS, &c.,
By the most esteemed makers, on SALE or HIRE.

MUSIC AT HALF-PRICE.
Proprietor—Mr. ASHE, (LATE PILBROW.)

THE MOST IMPAIRED SIGHT
Effectually restored by the aid of
SOLOMON'S SPECTACLES!
WHICH MAY BE OBTAINED AT
1, MARKET STREET,
Adjoining Fore Street and the Lower Market,
EXETER,
Being the only exclusive Spectacle Establishment in the West of England.

⁂ To prevent imposition, all Articles sold at the above Establishment will bear the mark of "*M. Solomon, Exeter.*"

Residence—3, Lansdowne Terrace.

Try the following Medicine for yourselves, and then to your neighbours give it the character it deserves. Strictly follow the directions, and the cure is certain, if at all curable.

ELLIS'S
FRIEND IN NEED,
OR
RHEUMATIC EMBROCADE,
MINT, EXETER,

In Bottles, at 1s. 1½d., each; and large ones containing three small, 2s. 9d.

The most speedy and effectual remedy ever yet discovered for Rheumatism, Rheumatic Gout, Lumbago, Sciatica, Ulcerated Sore Legs, Pains in the Limbs and Numbness, Stiffness in the Joints or Neck, Pains in the Face, Sprains or Bruises, Chilblains before broken, Bunions, Quinsey, Sore Throat, Asthma, Hooping Cough, and all external Inflammations.

CHARLES TITHERLEY,

HATTER,

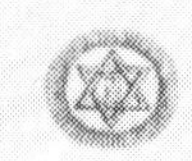

1, LONDON INN SQUARE,
Opposite the Royal Public Rooms,
EXETER.

LIVERY HATS, LACE, TRAVELLING CAPS, &c.

CATHEDRAL CLOSE SCHOOL, EXETER.

HEAD MASTER, MR. EDMUND T. FOWERAKER.

The object of this School, which has been primarily established for the Education of the Choristers of the Cathedral, is to ensure a sound English Commercial Education to the sons of the middle and business classes of society, as well as to those who may afterwards pursue a higher course at College or the Public Schools.

The Course of Education will embrace—Divinity, the Liturgy, Ecclesiastical History, Ancient and Modern History.

ENGLISH in all its Branches, including Reading, Grammar, Composition, Geography.

MATHEMATICS, comprising Arithmetic, Book-keeping, Mensuration, Algebra, Geometry, Plane Trigonometry.

The Elements of Greek and Latin.
Vocal Music.

The Terms for the above are—
For BOARDERS .... £25 per annum.
For DAY PUPILS under twelve years of age .... 4 Guineas per annum.
For DAY PUPILS above twelve years of age .... 6 Guineas per annum.

GERMAN, FRENCH, AND DRAWING ON THE USUAL TERMS.

The School Year is divided into four equal terms, ending respectively—MARCH 25th. JUNE 24th. SEPTEMBER 29th. DECEMBER 25th.

The Hours of Attendance are for Day Pupils, from 9 to 12, and from 2 to 5 o'clock.

The Holidays are three weeks at Christmas and four weeks at Midsummer.

Notice of removal of Pupils.—A quarter's notice is required previous to the removal of a Pupil.

Premises.—The School House (lately occupied as the Exeter Diocesan Training College,) has a play-ground attached, and ample accommodation for all the requirements of a Boarding School.

To the moral and religious training of the Pupils the utmost attention will be given. The Scriptures will be daily read in all the classes; and the School will each day begin and end with prayer.

Further Particulars will be given on application to the Head Master. *Cathedral Close, Exeter.*

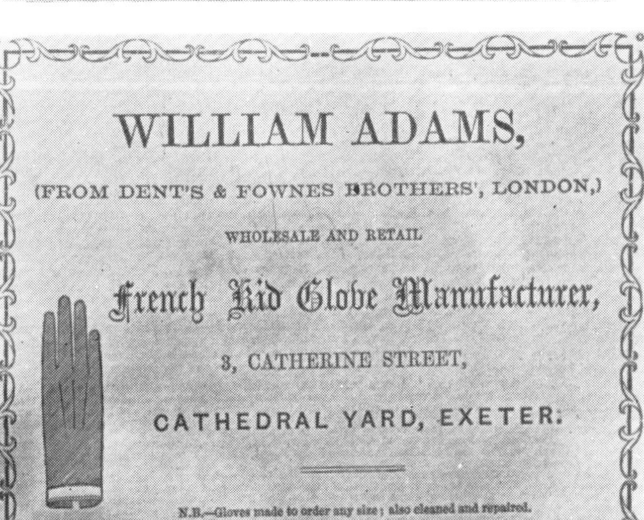

An assortment of old advertisements

More like a painting than a photograph, this delightful study was taken after the first world war. It shows the great activity and fun the frozen river created.

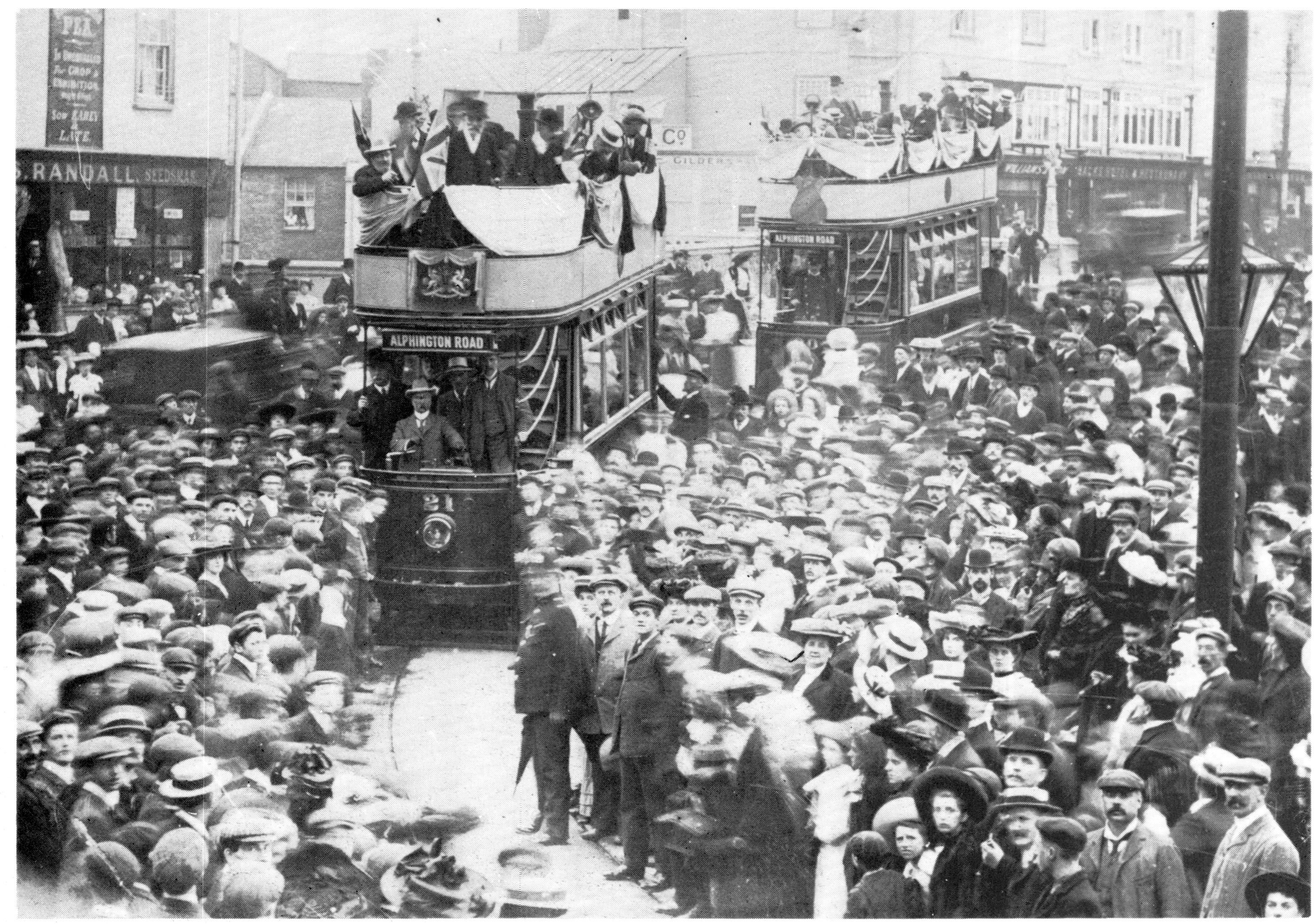

The first tram over the New Bridge, driven by the Mayor. The people appear to be more interested in the camera than the new trams.

Looking from Cowick Street over the New Bridge to Fore Street. (circa 1910)

Exeter Quay and Ferry. The crest shown on this page was photographed on one of the old warehouses (which date from 1835) standing on the quayside. The quay was designed to accommodate vessels entering the city via the canal.

An excellent example of early shipping at the Quay. This is the location used by the B.B.C. for their television series "The Onedin Line". Clearly shown in the background is the Custom House and to the right what is now the Prospect Inn. The two trading schooners tied up at quay capture the working atmosphere era and indeed a tremendous amount of trade was undertaken. Timber, coal, wine, spirits, wool and other products were loaded here and transported by sea. Photographed between 1870–1880.

A ship offloading at the lower quay. St. Leonards Church is in the left background. Down river, the old Match Factory can be seen in the distance. *(circa 1870.)*

The Wet Dock or Basin. This magnificent photograph illustrates well this essential part of the Exeter shipping system. Taken around 1870 by Bedford the photographer, it shows a topmast schooner tied up in the basin.

Formed at the head of the canal, the Basin accommodated vessels of considerable size. It was opened on the 29th of September 1830. Barges covered with streamers and filled with people travelled down to the Double Locks and back to the Basin, cheered by thousands of spectators. Afterwards, a grand dinner was held by the Exeter Chamber of Trade. Today, the Basin is the home of the Exeter Maritime Museum, housing a unique collection of world-wide craft.

The Annual Inspection of the Canal by the Council. (*circa 1880.*)

Exeter Canal is the oldest in Great Britain. Originally of narrow width, over the years it was improved so that ships of greater tonnage could navigate it. In 1827 another 3 miles were added at a cost of some £100,000. Being another opportunity for merriment, numerous vessels, barges and boats floated down to receive the first vessel to sail in. Unfortunately, troubles arose which prevented the ship from entering and it was a few days before the vessel came into Exeter. Thousands of spectators witnessed this event that was to herald greater prosperity for the City. Today the canal is only used commercially by one vessel and is otherwise for leisure pursuits only. The double lock was a popular resort and the rowing club celebrated its opening in 1904.

A typical Exeter tavern, Fred Pratt's Star and Garter on the corner of Bonhay Road. Further down Bonhay Road was the old cattle market. The pub obviously received a good deal of trade from country folk on market days.

Driving sheep to the Cattle Market in Bonhay Road. (circa 1900).
Entering Exeter and branching off from Exe Bridge to the left we are at the corner of Bonhay Road, where the Star and Garter was situated. The busy day for the Old Cattle Market in Bonhay Road was Friday, when cattle were regularly herded into the city. Bonhay Road Market saw the end of the era of the horse in Exeter, when the last of the magnificent council horses were sold.

A delightful character study, the shepherd in his traditional dress complete with bowler hat and crooked stick.

The end of a delightful era in Exeter, the selling of the council horses. The sale took place in the Bonhay Road Market and obviously attracted many spectators.

Fore Street viewed from the junction with West Street.

Walter Otton, Ironmonger

The main route leading into the city from the Exe Bridge is by way of Fore Street. As Exeter is situated on a hill Fore Street is rather steep, therefore with the arrival of steam engines and other vehicles it was not unusual for accidents to occur. My late uncle had such an experience with a runaway bus which he was driving The traction engine accident in 1906, shown above and the 1917 tram accident on the following page were typical of such incidents.

Henry Wykes the photographer captured the moment of disaster when the tram accident outside his studio in 1917 created great interest. His studio was directly behind the fallen tram.

WESTGATE

Coming from Fore Street down West Street we enter the West Quarter. Originally, the old West Gate of the city stood opposite the charming little church of St. Mary Steps. Unfortunately the Gate was removed in 1814. The whole of this area was chiefly inhabited by fullers, dyers, weavers and other trades needing proximity to water. Previously wealthy merchants had resided in this area, but with increasing fortune moved to larger houses.

Many of the old houses were converted to other uses. Today we are fortunate there still remains a most charming part of this quarter, much of which has been renovated.

During the period illustred on the following pages you see glimpses of the poverty that existed in the West Quarter.

The famous "Matthew The Miller" church clock shows the four seasons. The centre statue is of Henry VIII and it bends forward on the hour. On each side of Henry stands a soldier, both hold a javelin and a hammer with which they alternately strike the quarter hours. The name Matthew the Miller is derived from an old miller who was noted for his punctuality in visiting his customers at certain hours of the day.

A now famous and delightful setting in the West Quarter, at this time the most poverty stricken district in Exeter,(circa 1900)

St. Mary Steps Church viewed from another angle. The Church dates back to 1291, but the actual erection date is not known.

A detailed study of the statuette of Henry VIII, immediately above the "Matthew the Miller Clock".

The corner that was to see change and thereby make world wide news. The house in this picture was demolished and the famous Tudor House was put on wheels and brought to be positioned on the site on 12th December 1961.

Stepcott Hill, probably the most painted and sketched street in Exeter. An ancient street with a charm of it's own.

An alley off Stepcott Hill. Sad little faces show the hard life endured by the inhabitants of the West Quarter. This was an area where the police always patrolled in pairs. *(circa 1900)*

Typical of the area, Stepcott Hill had an open gutter running down the middle which was used as a playground by the children of the poor in the vicinity.

Higher Stepcott Hill showing a group of children in their playground! Most people living in the West Quarter would have been employed nearby; in weaving, dyeing, shipping and other industries in this part of the city.

Another picturesque corner of Exeter which was well loved by artists. The Tudor House on the left is the one which was wheeled uphill and re-sited by St. Mary Steps Church on 12th December 1961.

The Old Tudor House situated in Tudor Street, Exe Island, has been standing here for around 500 years, possibly dating back to 1450. The arms shown on the front of the house are those of Elizabeth Leach and John Gubbs. They are beautifully executed in scalloped slate and locally considered quite unique. The whole front was decorated in such fashion, but the upper is believed to have been destroyed around 1820.

[A] rare treat for some of the poor of Tuder Street, when the photographer paid a visit. The scalloped slate is shown more clearly here [t]han in the previous photograph. This building was left in a ruinous state until some 12 years ago, when a local builder purchased the [b]uilding and recently finished a meticulous and complete restoration at a very high personal cost. Amazingly all original timbers were [r]e-used and even the ancient nails were straightened and re-used. The actual cost of renovation was around £40,000. Owing to the high [c]ost incurred, the house was offered for sale to the Local Council, but due to the economic climate it was turned down. A Trust was [a]lso set up to keep the building, but owing to lack of support from the citizens it failed. It is now thought it will be converted into flats.

Tuckers Hall, Fore Street. A beautiful room of great antiquity and interest. Not too well known by many Exonians. *(circa 1930)*

A Tillet Block
(Used in Exeter in the 18th century).

TUCKERS HALL

Containing one of the most delightful rooms in Exeter and situated inconspicuously in the centre of Fore Street, Tuckers Hall is often missed by the passer-by. The hall dates from 1471 and belongs to the Company of Tuckers, Weavers and Shearmen, the last of Exeter's ancient Guilds which were created in 1490. The room is the same today as when this photograph was taken, and shows one of the finest examples of an oak panelled chamber that exists in England.

The hall is still used today on limited occasions by members and privileged guests. Being directly connected with the woollen industry we can see illustrated early tillet blocks used for marking the bales of wool. To outline their history we have printed on the next page an extract from an article in The Western Antiquary of July 1882, written by a Mr. Harry Hems of Exeter.

A Tillet Block
(Used in Exeter in the 18th century)

A Tillet Block
(Used in Exeter in the 18th century).

A Tillet Block
(Used in Exeter in the 18th century).

OLD TILLET BLOCKS

In the last century Exeter had, next to Leeds, the largest woollen market in the Kingdom. The trade had been connected with the former ancient city, and in the Parliamentary records of the beginning of the 16th century woollen goods from Exeter are frequently mentioned. At the commencement of the 18th century, it is said that the trade was so general, that eight out of every ten citizens were connected with it. In 1750 over 300,000 pieces of woollen goods, valued at one million pounds were exported from Exeter, yet, if we except the ancient Hall of the Tuckers, Weavers, and Shearmen and their Charities, we have little or nothing now to remind us of a great trade which has altogether passed away from our midst.

The illustrations on this and the previous page are prints from wooden blocks, which were at one time actively connected with Exeter's staple trade. They are the trade marks of merchants of the 18th century, and were used as distinguishing devices stamped upon bales of woollen goods – the cloth for exportation was wrapped in pieces of buckram – called "tillets" – and these stumps were known as tillet blocks. The making of the blocks was a speciality, and there is character about the few that yet remain, which goes to prove, that in spite of the non-existence of schools of art in those days, the art workman knew how to make bold, good lines, simple as they were in composition, but full of effect and power.

It seems that the trade mark was first put on the wraps in a showy colour by means of a stencil, and ultimately completed by the impression of the tillet block. This was printed on by a tillet press. Afterwards, when disused for this purpose, the old presses were adapted for ordinary type printing.

And this latter observation suggests the remark that the art of stamping impressions of religious subjects by wood was very probably the original suggestor of the whole art and mystery of printing.

The ups and downs of life are illustrated in those curious tillet blocks. The trade and the traders have gone; and these, the "trade marks" of the western merchants, are now of no monetary, but of historic value. Towards the end of the last century, my maternal grandfather, a Sheffield cutler named George Wostenholm, chose the three letters I.X.L., as a trade mark for his cutlery. Its market value at the present moment, protected by Act of Parliament from piracy, as are all marks pertaining to the Cutlers Company, is estimated at not less than £80,000, or over £25,000 a letter.

Harry Hems. Exeter.

Extracted from The Western Antiquary, July 1882.

Coming to the top of Fore Street, on the right hand side stood Milk Street. The photograph, taken during the festive season, shows street traders selling oranges at 6d. per pound and mistletoe hangs from a barrow on the left. The background clearly shows that this was a side street adjacent to the Old Lower Market or Corn Exchange. Unfortunately, the Old Market was blitzed and what remained was eventually demolished.

Cavalier's Houses. Two beautiful early seventeenth Century houses situated in upper Fore Street and according to Crockers Book of Old Exeter by far the best examples there were in this area. The first house was built in the reign of James I and the lower in that of Charles I. In 1886 Crocker notes that both were constructed of well seasoned British oak although internally nothing much remained of note, except for a good plaster ceiling. A most interesting point shown in these photographs is the gables. It will be seen that on the furthermost house in the next photograph there is a small statue of a man on a horse. The figure, it has been suggested, dates back to early civil wars. It indicated that the establishment was a place of entertainment, or a Cavalier's house, not to be frequented by those of the opposite persuasion.
A more common theory, is that these particular houses sheltered Prince Charles on his route to the west after the battle of Worcester. The figures of pottery being a signal to his friends, in order to denote Speed, however it appears that Charles never reached further west than Axminster.

The same building around 1910. The cavalier has reappeared on the roof. Reason not known.

The site, now known as "Winstons" was redeveloped after the war and nothing remains of the original buildings.

LLOYD'S CIGARETTE FACTORY

Situated in No. 76 and 77 Fore Street was the Cigarette factory of H. C. Lloyd, whose history stretched from 1784 to the early 1920's. The factory produced cigarettes, cigars, tobacco and snuff. The various products were marketed with some delightful brand names. Cigarettes for instance were called Tipsy Loo, Silver Fir, Lid Lals, Tinners Pipe Tobaccos, Prince Llewelyn Tre, Pol, and Pen 100 A1 at Lloyds.

Although this Company has fallen into obscurity, there is still something which retains its memory and that is the cigarette cards issued by Messrs. Lloyds. The factory employed a large number of women some of whom were duly photographed and presented on these cards. There were also other subjects chosen, such as famous Generals etc. The eventual closure of the factory was said to be due to the sending of free tobacco to the troops in France during the 1914–18 war. Later, it was taken over by Woolworths and then Exeter Corporation Electricity showrooms until it was blitzed in 1941.

loyds Cigarette Factory decorations proudly showing loyalty to Queen Victoria during the celebration of her Jubilee in 1897.

The corner of North Street and High Street. St. Peter's statue looks down at his book with business men relaxing below. (circa 1890)

HIGH STREET, CROSSROADS

At this spot we stand on the crossroads of High Street, Fore Street, South Street and North Street. The photograph on the previous page shows St. Peter's corner, so called because of the statue of St. Peter situated in the alcove on the corner of North Street. A poem about this famous statue goes as follows:-

When he hears the clock strike four, thumb's a leaf and turns it o'er and then reads on.

St. Peter stands on a pagan image.

Although this corner was considerably altered after the photograph was taken the statue still remains today in its corner position, now Hepworth's the Tailors.

The Butcher's shop, South Street. Trading today under new management. *(circa 1902)*

South Gate Plaque

Butchers Row

South Street's Butchery Establishment.
At the foot of South Street we have a fine example of late sixteenth or early seventeenth century work. For many years used as a butchers shop and still used today for the same purpose. It is interesting to note the open fronted shop and one can only imagine the problems they must have had with hot summer weather. The interior of this building has an exceptional plaster ceiling.

The Vicar's Choral, South Street, erected in 1387 by Bishop Brantingham. Also included in the building, was a kitchen and chambers for members of the College of Vicar's Choral who were required for services in the Cathedral. The house had numerous occupiers and was even owned by Henry VIII at one time. In 1847 it was purchased by the Dean and Chapter and then passed to the Ecclesiastical Commissioners. Sadly, it was totally destroyed in the war.

ALBERT E. WASSELL,

CHINA, GLASS AND EARTHENWARE

ESTABLISHMENT,

1, Queen Street, Exeter.

The Stock comprises everything that is new, of the most elegant designs, in *Dinner Dessert, Breakfast, Tea and Coffee Services.*

CHAMBER SETS

In all varieties, including some of the most unique patterns which skill and originality could devise, in shapes elegantly classical and ornamental.

ENGLISH AND FRENCH VASES, JARS,

CHINA AND ALABASTER GROUPS,

PARIAN NOVELTIES, GLASS SHADES, &c.

Particular attention is invited to the much improved *Ironstone China*, which for strength, durability, and moderate cost, stands unrivalled in *modern porcelain art.*

THE GLASS DEPARTMENT

Includes fine specimens of work, in Engraved and Cut *Decanters, Water Jugs and Goblets, Spirit Bottles, Centre Dishes, Claret Jugs, LUSTRES, Champagne, Claret, and Wine Glasses, Tumblers, Finger Basins, Wine Coolers, Butter Dishes, Sugar and Cream Basins,* and every requisite for the table of the most brilliant quality; at prices open to competition, and in accordance with the regulated economy of the times.

DINNER and other **SERVICES** made up in sets *of any size* to suit the convenience of purchasers: thus offering the advantage of matching *a single plate* or other piece, if broken, without delay.

Bread and Cheese Pans, Butter Jars, Salting Pans, Pickling and Preserving Pots, Gooseberry Bottles, and every description of common printed and coarse ware for kitchen use.

China and Glass on Hire. Matchings carefully attended to.

COUNTRY ORDERS EXECUTED WITH CARE AND ATTENTION.

Shopkeepers and the Trade supplied at the lowest wholesale prices.

RICH WEDDING CAKES.

WILLIAM CUTHBERTSON,

57, SOUTH STREET, EXETER,

Bread and Biscuit Baker, Cook, Confectioner, Pastry Cook, and Wedding Cake Manufacturer.

CONTRACTOR FOR WEDDING BREAKFASTS, BALL SUPPERS, AND FETES OF ANY KIND

Importer of French and Italian Confectionary.

Cream and Water Ices, Ice Puddings, Jellies, Blancmange, Creams, Trifles, Custards, Wafers Meringues, Sugar Work, Ornamental Vases, Baskets, French Pastry, and Savoy Cakes, Soups, Entrées, Potted Meats, Brawns, Perigord and Seasoned Pies and Rolls, Mince Pies, Patties, Lobster and other Salads, Puddings, Sweet Sandwiches, Tarts and Cheesecakes, Vol-au-Vents, Bonbons and Cosaques, Crystallised and other Fruits for Desserts, Preserves, Preserved Lemons and Oranges, Candied Lemon and Orange Peel, Chips and Rings, Comfits and all Sweets, Lozenges of every kind, Barley Sugar, Pink and White Candy, Dessert Papers, Presburg Wine Biscuits, Gateau de Brioche, Rice and Rout Cakes, Macaroons, Ratafias, Fruit and Seed Cakes, Ginger Wafer Biscuits, Christening and School Cakes, every assortment of Biscuits, Gingerbread of every description, Sago and Arrow-root Cakes, Tops and Bottoms, Norwich Rusks and Biscuit Powder for Infants' Food.

Breakfast and Dinner Bread, Luncheon Cakes, Muffins, Sally-Luns, French Rolls, Cakes, Twists, &c., Household, Meal, and Milk Bread, daily.

'AYMES'

WRAP" LEGGINGS.

The new "Wrap" is the greatest improvement in Gaiters ever invented.

"MEOPHAM.

"The Leggings are quite the best fit and "shape I have ever had made anywhere. "The method of fastening is simplicity "itself.—W.M.B."

It is the simplest and most comfortable to wear, is very smart and clean, unsurpassable for walking and riding, will not tear open in the jungle, is unique, and does not tire. It will soon supersede all other leggings for Military, Sporting, and Colonial wear. Made in any Leather.

All kinds of Strap, Lace and Button Seamless Leggings.

F. HAYMES, Military & Sporting Bootmaker,

1, BEDFORD STREET, EXETER.

THOMAS MAY.

ENGLISH AND FRENCH

BOOT & SHOE WAREHOUSE,

75, FORE STREET, EXETER.

Local traders advertise their wares

An Aerial view of Exeter's most dominant building, the Cathedral stands majestically in the centre of the City. Photographed in 1927.

The West Front of the Cathedral (Circa 1930)

EXETER CATHEDRAL

In the centre of Exeter stands one of the finest Cathedrals in England. Boasting a history of 1,000 years and some of the finest architectural design of early periods. Many books have been written about this magnificent structure. However, we can only touch briefly on the history of this building which today attracts people from all over the world.

Our photographs show; aerial views of the Cathedral and the two great Norman Towers, the 14th Century West Front Window and the Cathedral when it was first illuminated. Another, when the West Window was boarded up for protection during the war years against bomb blast and fortunately no damage occurred to the West Front. Interior photographs show the magnificent nave, stretching over 300 feet and the longest in Europe. In the middle of the nave is situated the splendid Cathedral organ which was built in 1665, front and rear views are shown. Walking down the nave and looking up we see the Minstrels Gallery where the choir boys sing at Christmas – Voices Heavenwards!

Some years ago the public were allowed to walk in the Bishop's gardens at the rear of the Cathedral. Today this practice has stopped and so the public miss some of the beautiful rear views of the Cathedral with the adjacent Bishop's Palace and Norman Tower in the background.

The Cathedral bells which have rung out over the city for centuries have a fascinating history in themselves. In the South Tower there is the heaviest ringing peal of bells in the world, consisting of twelve bells. The tenor bell weighs 72 cwt and is called the Grandisson Bell, after Bishop Grandisson from whom it was a gift to the Cathedral. In the North Tower one bell hangs alone, Great Peter, weighing 125 cwt and dating back to 1484. In 1902 some of the bells were recast and as the next photograph shows aroused a certain amount of interest and earnest conversation. Probably as to how the bell was to be got back up the tower!

The Cathedral, a magnificent piece of human craftsmanship is without doubt Exeter's greatest possession, and long may we hope it will remain so.

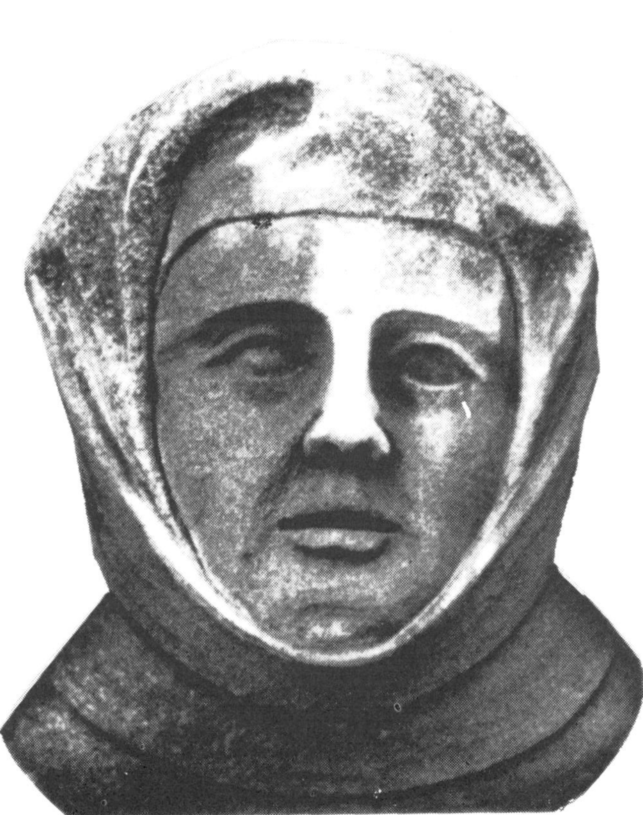

After recasting, one of the Cathedral Bells awaiting to be rehung in readiness for the Coronation of King Edward VII. Date 1902.

The illuminated West Front of the Cathedral showing the bomb blast screen still in place. The great window had to be protected as much as possible during the war. Luckily the Cathedral escaped with only slight damage.

Gargoyle Photos

More Cathedral Gargoyles

The magnificent nave looking east. The interior is the finest of its type in England and indeed greatly assists Exeter Cathedral's reputation as one of the finest in Europe.

The Organ which dates from 1665 and was made by John Loosemore. The tonal quality of the instrument is superb and cannot fail to impress the listener.

' rear view of the great organ, a masterpiece of craftsmanship. In front of the organ in this view are the choir stalls.

The Minstrel's Gallery, where an annual attraction is the singing of the choir boys at Christmas.

Captain Robert Falcon Scott the famous Devonshire explorer is remembered in Exeter Cathedral. In a quiet corner of the nave hangs the flag that accompanied Captain Scott on his expedition to the South Pole. The photograph shown was presented to Sir Peter Scott by the Isca Collection. The son of the famous explorer, Sir Peter Scott has also achieved fame, but in the field of nature conservation and is the chairman of The World Wild Life Fund.

The entrance to the Bishop's Palace and in the background the South Tower. At one time the Bishop's garden was open to the general public, but sadly the privilege has been withdrawn.

An early record of the West Front illuminated.

From the air the gothic roof of the Cathedral can easily be observed. The vaulted gothic structure extends over 300 feet and is claimed to be the finest example of its type in Europe.

Civic dignitaries lead a long procession to the Cathedral to celebrate the Cathedral's Octocentenary. On the left of the obelisk stands the Globe Hotel which was destroyed by incendaries during the war.

The procession leaves the Cathedral and the event is recorded by a gentleman using a hand cranked cine camera.

CATHEDRAL CLOSE

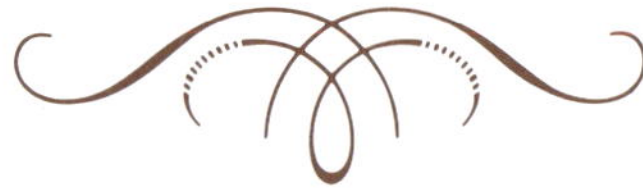

This famous and picturesque part of the Cathedral Close shows St. Martins Church, Mol's Coffee House and adjacent shops. (Circa 1890)

St. Martins Church has a very ancient history and dates back to 1065. The shop next door, the most delightful in Exeter, is Mol's Coffee House. Around 1590 this was owned by an Italian, a certain Mr. Mol, who prospered by offering his establishment for refreshments. It was here that the Military and Naval gentlemen met to discuss the battle against the Spanish Armada.

In the room on the first floor the walls are panelled in oak and contain 46 coats of arms on small shields approximately 6 inches square. During the period shown Mol's Coffee house was occupied by Worth & Co. frame makers, picture cleaners and photographers. This company produced some delightful work and helped to record the City with their etchings and postcards.

A closer look at Mol's Coffee House and St. Martins Church. (Circa 1900)

Just off Cathedral Close is Catherine Street and this is an early record of the street. Date unknown.

Catherine Street – 1890. Showing a more prosperous and much improved state to that illustrated in the previous photograph.

Situated next door to the Royal Clarence Hotel the Exeter Bank opened on 9th July 1769. In 1902 the bank amalgamated and afterwards Dellers Cafe occupied the building. At a later date it was to become part of the Clarence Hotel. Exeter bank notes were displayed on the walls of the Hotel. In St. Martins Lane, to the right of the bank stands the Ship Inn, a favourite haunt of Sir Francis Drake. A noted saying of Sir Francis was, "Next to mine own shippe I do most prefer the olde shippe in Exon".

ROYAL CLARENCE HOTEL

Of all the hotels in Exeter the Royal Clarence in the Cathedral Close is probably the best known. Its central situation overlooks the Cathedral Green. This fine building was erected in 1770 when the first landlord was a Frenchman Peter Berlon – hence the name hotel, derived from the french 'hote'. In the early days it was always referred to as 'The Hotel' in the churchyard and was then the first hotel in England.

In 1806 Jenkins History of Exeter contained the following recommendation. The only house, worthy of notice in its parish is, The Hotel, a large commodious Inn, with elegant apartments and Hotel accommodation for people of the first quality, with a large assembly room in which the assize balls, concerts and assemblies of the most distinguished persons of City and Country take place, in the front is a neat coffee room. The situation of 'The Hotel' is very pleasant as it opens to the parade and commands a noble view of the Cathedral. In 1815 a meeting was held in the Clarence to discuss the lighting of Exeter by gas. It was to be the first place in the County to receive gas for lighting.

One of the most famous people to visit the Clarence was Horatio Nelson in 1801. He was made an Honorary Freeman of the City and after a grand reception at the Guildhall returned to 'The Hotel'.

Having a long history The Hotel boasted a fine collection of antiques. Unfortunately, I understand that many of the most valuable and interesting disappeared after changes of ownership. The collection is somewhat smaller today, but not so many years ago 468 pieces were listed.

The Cathedral Tower commands an interesting view over the Royal Clarence Hotel to Queen Street. It is interesting to note how buildings were far more compacted than they are today.

H. J. Weaver,

Ostrich Feather Cleaner,

4, St. Olave's Square,

EXETER.

NOTE.—All orders received by post not later than Wednesday morning are returned by Saturday morning of the same week.

SCHOLASTIC.

MISS E. G. BUDGE'S

Ladies' School and Musical Academy,

SIDWELLA LODGE,

Nearly opposite the Church,

SIDWELL ST., EXETER.

TERMS.

For French, Music, and Drawing, (practical and theoretical,) combined with the usual educational routine, Six Guineas per annum.

A sound English education, without accomplishments, Two Guineas per annum.

W. J. J. NORTON'S

Devon and Exeter Wholesale and Retail

GUTTA PERCHA DEPOT,

81, SIDWELL STREET, EXETER.

MILL BANDS—more durable and 50 per cent. cheaper than Leather.

TUBING—for Watering Gardens—for the conveyance of Beer, Water, Chemicals, &c.—for Speaking Tubes in Warehouses, Counting Houses, and Public Institutions, and Hearing Apparatus for the Deaf in Churches and Chapels.

THIN SHEET—(a substitute for Oiled Silk), useful for Surgical purposes, lining for Bonnets, Dresses, &c.

REFINED WHITE GUTTA PERCHA for filling Decayed Teeth.

Railway Conversation Tubes
Ear Trumpets
Window Blind and Sash Cord
Toilet Services
Whips
Drinking Cups
Life Buoys
Photographic Trays and Baths
Curtain Rings, Funnels
Picture Frames and Mouldings
Fancy Baskets
Card and Fruit Trays
Inkstands, Candlesticks
Vases, Watchstands
Chessmen and Draughts

And a unique assortment of Fancy Articles.

☞ For Comfort! Durability!! and Economy!!! wear the Patent GUTTA PERCHA SOLES AND OVERSHOES, which keep the Feet warm and dry, and are indispensable to all who value Health.

☞ PATENT VULCANIZED INDIA-RUBBER WAREHOUSE.

Six Shirts for 24s.,

Made of good Materials and superior Needlework, to be had at

JOHN SPALDING'S

OUTFITTING WAREHOUSE,

32, High Street, Exeter, 32,

Where also will be found a Large and Fashionable Stock of

FANCY, FLANNEL, AND SPUN SILK SHIRTS,

Once-round Scarfs, Neckerchiefs, Bandannas, Albert Ties, Mufflers,

Cambridge, Piccadilly, and Military Shirt Collars,

Braces, Lamb's-Wool, Merino, and Segovia Under Shirts and Drawers, Hose, Half-Hose, Umbrellas, &c., &c.

OUTFITS TO INDIA AND THE COLONIES

Executed with punctuality and economy.

32, High Street, Exeter. 32.

J. PHILLIPS,

COACH BUILDER,

&c.,

EAST SOUTHERNHAY,

THREE DOORS BELOW THE BARNFIELD,

EXETER.

H. P. DICKER,

ORGAN BUILDER;

MANUFACTORY, GANDY STREET, EXETER.

H. P. DICKER begs respectfully to inform the Nobility and Clergy, that having been for many years practically engaged in Organ building, he is enabled through personally superintending the fitting-up of his Instruments, to warrant what work leaves his manufactory to be of the best materials and workmanship, and to execute orders at a moderate charge.

H. P. D. having hitherto given general satisfaction to those who have honoured him with their orders, and having been engaged in almost every part of the country, either in erecting or improving Organs, confidently hopes that those who may hereafter employ him will experience the same satisfaction.

The following is a list of a few of the Instruments which he has built for Churches and Chapels:—
Upton Church, Torquay, containing 38 stops, which was opened by Dr. Wesley, at the Royal Public Rooms, January, 1851.

Testimonial, by Dr. Wesley.

"My opinion being required of the qualities of the Organ just completed by Mr. Dicker, I have the pleasure to mention that it possesses decided merit, and I must add that I do not recollect ever to have given two lengthy public performances on a new Instrument, without the mechanism suffering a disarrangement, from which Mr. Dicker's Organ wholly escaped."

S. S. WESLEY.

Upton Church, Torquay
St. Mary's Church, Barbadoes, West Indies
Sidmouth Church
Wesleyan Chapel, Torquay
North Huish Church
Newton Bushell Church
Newton Abbot Church
East Teignmouth Church
Buckland Monachorum Church
Lympstone Church
Woodbury Church
Sir Trayton Drake, Two Instruments
General Lee, Two Instruments
Cheriton Bishop Church
Newton St. Cyres Church
South Tawton Church
Chagford Church
Moreton Hampstead Church
Dunsford Church
Up Ottery Church
Institution for the Blind
Halberton Church
Pilton Church, Barnstaple
Bishop's Tawton Church
Yeo Vale, near Bideford
Free Church, Ilfracombe
St. George's Church, Tiverton
Bradninch Church
Yarcombe Church
Whimple Church
St. Philip's Church, Barbadoes, West Indies
Independent Chapel, Tiverton
&c., &c., &c.

HARE'S

PINE'S DEVONSHIRE OILS,

FOR HORSES, SHEEP, CATTLE, &c.,

Are adapted both for external and internal use; and when judiciously used, will save the purse of the Farmer. They are admirably adapted for Sheep; and in cases of swelled udder, are unequalled.

The Proprietor refers his agricultural and other friends to the undermentioned persons, who can vouch for the efficacy of the Oils.

Mr. JNO. BEER, Yeoman, Newton Poppleford.
THOS. YELVERTON, Esq., Ven-Ottery.
Mr. FROOM, Yeoman, Sowton.
Mr. GEO. POOK, Yeoman, Whimple.
Mr. JNO. SATTERLY, Dairyman, New Town, Exeter.

Sold in Bottles, with Directions for Use, at 9d. and 1s. 9d. each.

MANGE LOTION, PHYSIC, CORDIAL, DIURETIC, AND OTHER BALLS, AND EVERY DESCRIPTION OF MEDICINE, PREPARED BY

W. HARE, Chemist & Druggist,

OPPOSITE THE HORSE BAZAAR,

21, PARIS STREET, EXETER.

MRS. ALBERT ADAMS,

MILLINERY, LACE, MUSLIN,

AND

CORSET ESTABLISHMENT,

234, HIGH STREET, EXETER,

(Opposite St. Stephen's Church.)

A choice selection of MILLINERY of every description.

A large assortment of MOURNING BONNETS always on hand.

FRENCH FLOWERS, RIBBONS, LACE AND MUSLIN GOODS, &c., &c., in great variety.

HILL'S PATENT CORSETS,

The most simple fastening and best shape invented.

MOURNING AND WEDDING ORDERS

CAREFULLY EXECUTED.

ROBERT REYNOLDS,

11, PARIS STREET, EXETER,

UPHOLSTERER,

CABINET MAKER,

AND

UNDERTAKER,

APPRAISER & HOUSE AGENT,

11, Paris Street, Exeter.

A selection of general advertisements.

The Guildhall, Exeter. Dating back to 1330 this is reputed to be the oldest Municipal building in the United Kingdom. The knife grinder in the left foreground appears to have an interested audience.

The reading of the proclamation of King George V outside the Guildhall.

EXETER GUILDHALL

Another civic treasure dating back to before the 12th century, Exeter's Guildhall stands prominent in the centre of High Street. It is said that the Guildhall is the oldest civic building in the Country. The present structure was rebuilt in 1330 and the hall re-roofed in 1466. Walking into the fine building you pass through a studded door of solid oak made in 1593. For many years the Guildhall was used as an Assize Court.

Naturally, the Guildhall has been the centre of all civic events presided over by the Mayor in Office. Paintings of some of these distinguished gentlemen hang in the Guildhall Chambers. Within the ancient building lies the city regalia, a priceless treasure, of great antiquity.

Under the portico of the Guildhall the stocks were sited. Drunkards were frequently locked in them and left to sober up! Fortunately this has now been discontinued. It is interesting to note that underneath the portico and still fixed in the ceiling is a large hook. This was used to suspend the public scales for the weighing of meat. The pork Butchers shambles covered this part of High Street from Goldsmith Street to Broadgate. The meat was weighed by one of the Guildhall Staff Bearers. Also, goods were deposited in the open reception area of the Guildhall, which is now the Guildhall attendants office.

The Guildhall and High Street in 1880. In these earlier years of Exeter, shop blinds were a most attractive feature and the pole holes can still be seen in some places today. Note the tiny church of Allhallows next to Newman's Central Stores. A church occupied this site as early as 1191. Allhallows was demolished in 1906.

J. Hinton Lake, Dispensing Chemist's shop, long established in this very old building. A popular family business which started around 1870, it also specialised in photographic pursuits. The milk cart outside the shop adds to the interest of this everyday scene in old Exeter.

A slightly later photograph of No. 41 High Street, this delightful building in central High Street situated opposite Queen Stree dates back to around 1566. Humourously, it is thought that the houses were designed with overhanging eaves to protect pedestrian from stormy weather.
It will be noted that the shop on the right hand side of the building which was the Gospel Depot and Publishing Co., when th previous photograph was taken, has now changed and is the Cycle Depot.

Looking up High Street from the Guildhall circa 1885. Muddy streets were typical and this photograph illustrates to some extent the conditions of the period.

Our cover photograph. The great change begins. Here we see the approaching end of the era of the horse and the beginning of the domination of the four wheeled version of horse-power; the motor car.

The bustling modern age has arrived and the traffic jams up outside Colsons one of Exeter's most exclusive shops. This photograph was used for the Mayor's Christmas Card in 1976.

Back to the age of the horse drawn carriage and another look at Queen Street.

Queen Street and Market, Exeter.

EXETER MARKETS

Before the Higher and Lower Markets were built in Exeter, street markets were held in High Street and Fore Street on Tuesdays and Fridays. Alternate sides of the street were used at six month durations. The big market days took place on the last Friday in the month and they created chaos because there was not enough room for coaches and carriages to pass.

Country people flocked to the markets and brought goods to sell. Grocers' shops acted as depositories for country fare and were piled high with baskets of goods.

The Higher Queen Street market as we know it today was opened on July 24th 1838. This of course helped to clear the streets and dealt with fish, potatoes and oats, together with dairy produce and vegetables. The market has not been used for a number of years, but has recently been restored although reduced in size and adapted as part of a new shopping centre in Exeter.

Mary Brooks – A County Carrier

The lady in this photograph is my great great grandmother. She was a carrier between Brampford Speke and Exeter, and walked there and back every day. Coming in on the Cowley Bridge Road she joined some 3,000 persons who came in to sell their goods on Friday Market days. Mary was apparently quite a character in Exeter and often had flagons of gin taken by children from her donkey cart on her way home. When she died the Express & Echo published a short poem to her memory. 'Mary had a little moke it's coat was rough but sleek, although a word he never spoke he lived at Brampford Speke'. The donkey lived for a number of years after her death and ended it's life at Rewe, Near Exeter.

The Museum, Queen Street and a passing tram.

Part of the Peel Collection as it was displayed in the Royal Albert Memorial Museum.

Peel the big game hunter sits in the middle of some of his trophies. The photograph was taken in Exeter around 1930.

Mr. Jenkins, Haulier, aiding removals from the Museum (Circa 1910)

The junction of Queen Street and Northernhay Street. Walking up to the left we enter Northernhay Gardens and to the right Northernhay Street where we come to the Iron Bridge erected in 1834, which spans the gap between North Street and St. Davids Hill. (Circa 1910)

Erected in 1897, The Clock Tower, Queen Street replaced the Quadrangle that stood in the same position. Both provided drinking facilities for horses as can be seen. The stone masons, Eastons of Exeter, erected the Tower and purchased a camera to capture their work for posterity. The camera, made by Walter Lawley, is shown on the next page and is now in my possession. It was saved from the dustcart!

Situated at the bottom of Queen Street the Quadrangle, which was to be replaced by the Clock Tower. The Clock Tower was erected from funds made available by Mrs. Miles, of Dixies Field. It was dedicated to the memory of her husband, who was devoted to the welfare of animals in the city. At the opening in 1898 Mrs. Miles was driven in a carriage pulled by two magnificent greys. These animals were the first to drink from the new troughs. On numerous occasions the Clock Tower has been the subject of attack by critics who claimed it was a traffic hazard. Recently the tower looked as though it was to disappear for good. However, it was saved by the Ministry Of The Environment who proclaimed it a building of special architectural interest.

A portrait of General Redvers Buller

GENERAL SIR REDVERS BULLER VC GCB GCMG

General Redvers Buller was born at Downes, Near Crediton in 1839. At the age of 18 he joined the Kings Own Rifles and embarked on a magnificent military career. It can be said that he was to become probably the most famous soldier ever to come from the West Country.

A man of great character, strength and precision he was to be renowned in his own lifetime.

The first major battle in which he participated was the Chinese War of 1860. Later he was to move to Canada and fought in the Red River Campaign in 1867 and again in 1873 in the Ashanti war he fought for his country. The year 1878 brought him to South Africa where his most heroic actions were to take place. Great battles in Egypt also saw his presence.

Although he spent most of his life in a military capacity for a short period in his life he returned to Downes, where he pursued farming activities. General Buller succeeded not only on the battlefield but in farming circles, it was a fact that he possessed some of the finest stock in the county. Certainly no one had finer horses for which he had a famous reputation.

To the local folk he was known as the Squire of The Downes.

Redvers Buller died in 1901 and it was decided that a statue should be erected to his memory in both Exeter and Plymouth. A home was also to be opened for wounded soldiers at Crediton. A shilling fund was opened, but got off to a poor start. However, after a large donation was obtained the general response improved. Money came from all parts of the world. On September 6th 1905 his statue was unveiled in Exeter by the Lord Lieutenant of Devon Viscount Ebrington. Today it still stands outside Bury Meadow.

MEDALS PRESENTED TO GENERAL BULLER

CHINA 1860	2 clasps
CANADA 1866–70	3 clasps
ASHANTI 1873	1 clasp
SOUTH AFRICA 1878–9	Victoria Cross
EGYPT 1882	4 clasps
JUBILEE MEDAL	
SOUTH AFRICA 1889–1901	6 clasps

Victoria Cross

The grand procession on its way to the unveiling of General Buller's statue on the 6th September 1905.

Part of the large crowd which gathered to commemorate the unveiling of the statue.

Exeter pays tribute to it's hero, General Redvers Buller. The statue was unveiled by Viscount Ebrington.

General Sir Redvers Buller's Memorial Card

General Buller on horse

Queen Victoria at the time of her Diamond Jubilee

Exeter's North Gate was demolished in 1769 and to celebrate Queen Victoria's Diamond Jubilee it was reconstructed in wood and plaster.

The young Queen Victoria

The commemorative stone which wa placed on the site of the Old North Ga on the occasion of Queen Victoria Diamond Jubilee.

Manufacturers were not slow to show their Royal Patronage and at the same time lay claims to the supremacy of their products

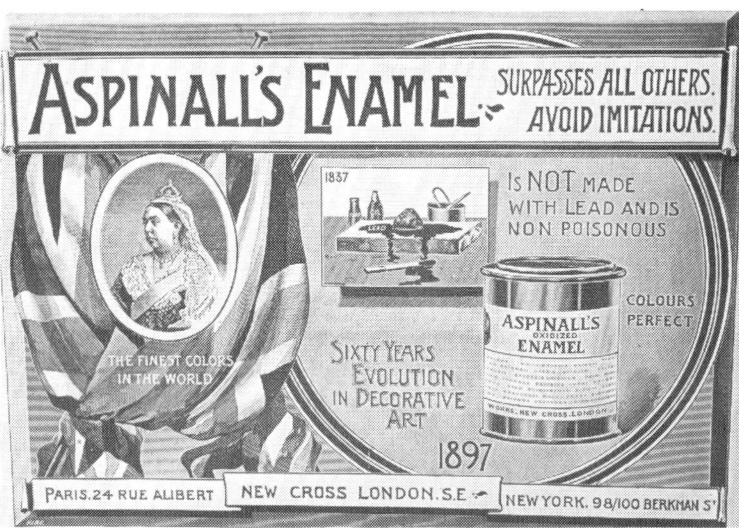

To add a further touch to the Jubilee celebrations South Gate was reconstructed in South Street. At one time South Street was only sixteen feet wide.

An early view of High Street by Frith, a well known photographer. Taken long before the tram or car arrived in Exeter, giving it a more rural feeling, with the stage-coach clattering down the street passing the Cathedral Dairy and the London Inn Square. *(Circa 1885)*

Another early view of High Street showing the Guildhall in a central position. This photograph was also taken by Frith, producer of Postcards from all over the country.

THE ANCIENT HOUSE OF "ROSS", HIGH STREET

Without doubt the finest example of 17th Century craftsmanship left in Exeter, the house dates from around 1650 and was probably built by a wealthy merchant. It appears that this building has been maintained in a very careful manner. However, in the last few years considerable alterations have taken place on this corner, the ground floor facades have been removed and replaced by modern shop fronts. The interior of the building was completely gutted and destroyed, and although of a much later period much character was destroyed with the modern replacement.

A delightful study of two of Exeter's famous old houses, with the house of Ross on the right.

Well known in Old Exeter, The Devon and Somerset Stores has opened its Xmas Bazaar. The horse drawn cabs await fares. It appears that there are no people in the street, but because of the camera's slow shutter speed pedestrians movements have not been arrested, therefore it is not unusual to see empty streets in early photographs.

An advertisement for Deller's Cafe, scene of Exeter's social whirl, with its String Orchestra and Dainty Afternoon Teas.

Another picture of Deller's Cafe, an excellent view of the interior of this romantic building.

BEDFORD CIRCUS

Formerly, the site of Bedford Circus was occupied by a Dominican Monastery. At the Dissolution in 1538 it was granted to Lord John Russell, who then converted it into a spacious dwelling. In 1773 it was demolished and Bedford Circus was constructed. Fourteen magnificent houses completed the circle together with an episcopal chapel. Unfortunately the total structure was lost in the blitz.

On this site in 1880 Lord Courtenay's statue was erected, attended by gentry, noblemen, and persons of high rank.

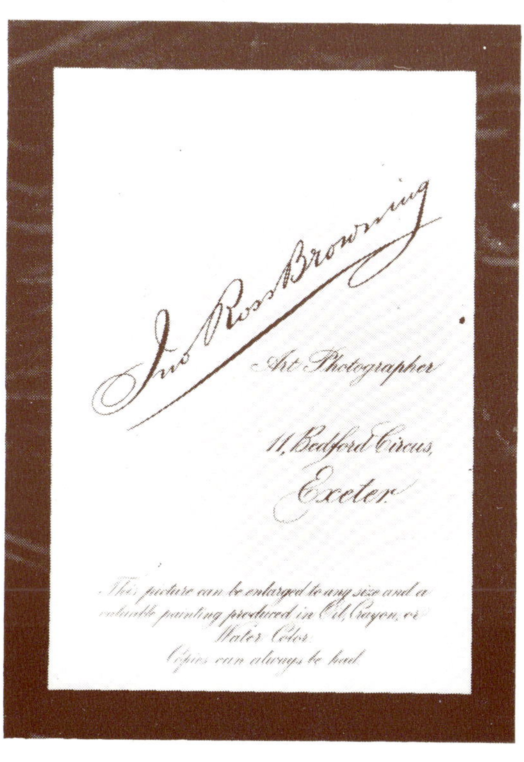

The erection of Lord Courtenay's statue in Bedford Circus on 8th October 1880, attended by Civic dignitaries and the local gentry.

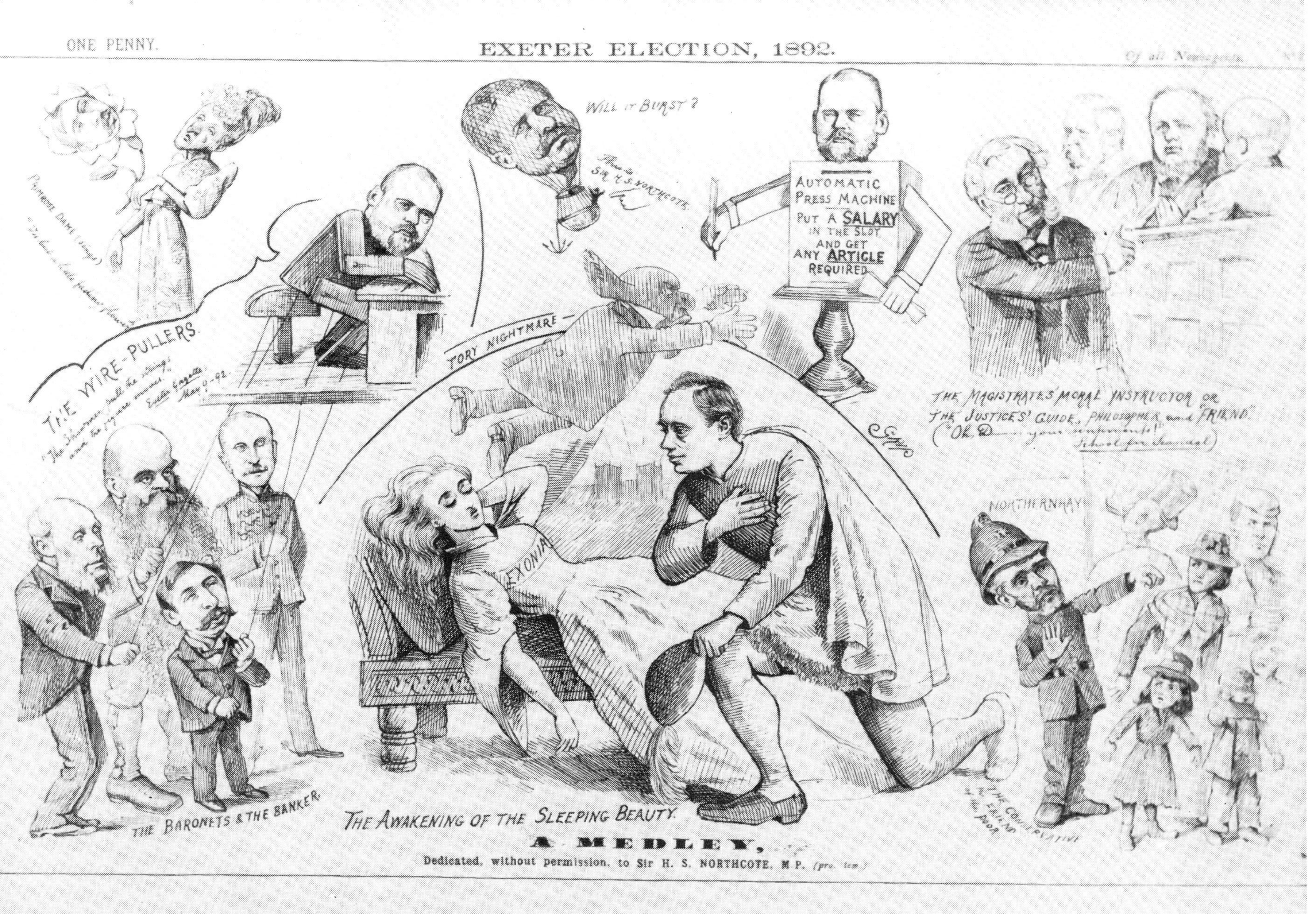

Exeter has always had an active political life and here you can see the type of political poster used in Elections in the late 19th Century.

A gathering of gentlemen's automobiles at the Half Moon Hotel on the corner of Bedford Street.

The Royal Devon and Exeter Hospital, Southernhay. Established in 1740 by Dr. Alfred Clarke, Dean of Exeter. The hospital had numerous benefactors to make it a substantial Medical Centre in the South West. The more priviledged patients arrived and hopefully, departed by carriage. (Circa 1900)

Burning clothes on Exe Island. The fences known as racks were used for drying and stretching woollens during the days of the flourishing wool trade.

Carrying the dead across the Exe Bridge.

THE CHOLERA EPIDEMIC OF 1832

Removal of dead from the West Quarter while a man washes bedding at the leat.

A body being carried from Mary Arches Street.

Odd neighbours in High Street. The local travel agents office advertising "Bottled Sunshine" and the "Paragon" Umbrella Shop.

JOHN HAWKINS,

Laceman, Hosier, Glover,

HABERDASHER, &c.,

11, High Street, Exeter, 11,

(Nearly opposite Castle Street.)

A BEAUTIFUL SELECTION OF

LACE AND MUSLIN COLLARS, SLEEVES, SETS, &C.,

HEAD DRESSES

In great variety, and made in any style to suit the wearer.

MILLINERY AND MANTLE ROOMS.

MOURNING AND WEDDING ORDERS

Carefully and promptly attended to.

HUXHAM'S & BROWN,

Ironfounders and Millwrights,

EXETER.

MACHINERY, STEAM ENGINES,

AGRICULTURAL MACHINES,

Millstones and French Burrs.

SHIP WORK, PATENT WINDLASS PURCHASES.

COOKING STOVES, GRATES,

WEIGHING MACHINES.

Malt Mills. Emigrants' Flour Mills.

Castings in general. Flour Mills and Machinery.

HUXHAM'S & BROWN,

Commercial Road,

Near the Quay, EXETER.

THE NEW ESTABLISHMENT

For the Manufacture and Sale of

Ladies' & Gentlemen's Boots & Shoes,

149, FORE STREET, EXETER,

(Opposite the Star Hotel.)

JAMES GILLHAM

Invites attention to his extensive and excellent Stock, which comprises every article from the most fashionable and highly finished to the plainest manufacture, where strength and durability are only required.

THE STOCK OF

READY-MADE BOOTS AND SHOES

Is large, and contains every requisite, and all Goods are warranted equal to bespoke—Wholesale Prices!

TREWMAN'S

Exeter Flying Post,

The principal Conservative Newspaper in the West of England.

TO ADVERTISERS.

The attention of the Legal Profession, of Surveyors, Auctioneers, Railway Companies, County Magistrate Commissioners of Turnpike Trusts, Guardians of Poor Law Unions, Insurance Companies, and other Public Bodies of Agriculturists, Merchants, Tradesmen, &c., who require a *valuable advertising medium*, is respectfully requeste to the following statistics of Newspaper Circulation, compiled from the latest Government Returns for *six month*

Trewman's Exeter Flying Post 70,000

Woolmer's Exeter Gazette	53,000	Hampshire Chronicle	26,800	Bath Gazette	13,00
Exeter Luminary	6,500	North Devon Journal	26,500	Bath Herald	10,00
Cornwall Gazette	30,000	Plymouth Mail	44,000	Bridgewater Times	10,00
Cornish Telegraph	9,250	Plymouth Journal	36,000	Somerset County Gazette	21,30
Devonport Independent	16,000	Plymouth Herald	16,000	Somerset Herald	16,00
Devonport Telegraph	25,000	Plymouth Times	3,000	Sherborne Journal	36,00
Dorset County Chronicle	29,000	Poole Herald	14,000	Torquay Directory	16,00
Hampshire Advertiser	68,500	Bath Chronicle	41,500	Torquay Chronicle	3,50
Hampshire Independent	34,367	Bath Journal	30,000	Wn. Flying Post (Yeovil Times)	32,00

It will be seen from the foregoing Official Returns that the *Exeter Flying Post* takes the lead of twenty-eight o the principal Newspapers in the Western Counties.

The *Flying Post* circulates amongst the Clubs and principal Hotels in London, and is to be found in the New Rooms and Hotels of the leading Provincial Towns in this Kingdom.

Since the repeal of the advertisement duty the charge for advertisements has been very much reduced, as the following brief extract from the scale indicates:—3 lines, 1s. 6d.; 4, 2s.; 5 and 6, 2s. 6d.; 7 and 8, 3s.; 9 and 10, 3s. 6d. 11 and 12, 4s.; with a proportionate increase for additional length.

A liberal reduction on the above rate of charges when advertisements are ordered for a series of three or si months.

Special contracts entered into with those who advertise continuously.

A specimen copy of the paper sent on receipt of five postage stamps.

Published every WEDNESDAY at Noon, and forwarded the same day to all parts of the Kingdom, by R. J. TREWMAN and CO., 226, High Street, Exeter.

MRS. J. T. TUCKER'S

MILLINERY, LACE, MUSLIN, AND BABY LINEN ESTABLISHMENT,

243, HIGH STREET, EXETER, 243,

Opposite the Half Moon Hotel.

Chemisettes, Habit Shirts and Sleeves

LACE JACKETS,

LACE AND MUSLIN COLLARS AND CAPES;

In this branch of trade MRS. TUCKER *has facilities for obtaining all* NOVELTIES,

COIFFURES,

FRENCH FLOWERS AND RIBBONS,

SILK APRONS, POCKET AND NECKERCHIEFS,

NECK TIES, SASHES, ARMLETS,

&c., &c.

ELEGANT FRENCH HEAD DRESSES.

An admirable stock of

BABY LINEN

always on hand, comprising

INFANTS' ROBES, CLOAKS, HOODS,

PELISSES, HATS, BONNETS,

GLOVES AND SOCKS,

With every variety of article necessary for Children, including BASSINETTS and NURSERY BASKETS, all on the most reasonable terms.

THE SHOW ROOMS

ARE REPLETE WITH ELEGANT

MANTLES, MILLINERY, AND CHILDREN'S DRESSES

Every article pertaining to a Lady's Trousseau completed with taste, promptitude, and economy.

S. PYNE,

146, FORE STREET HILL, 146

EXETER,

(Established 22 Years,)

BRUSH, MOP, PATTEN, CLOG AND COMB MANUFACTURER.

Dealer in Mats, and Sheffield Goods, Wholesale and Retail.

Tortoiseshell Combs repaired and altered to any pattern, or taken in Exchange.

SHOPKEEPERS SUPPLIED.

A further selection of advertisements of bygone days.

An excellent photograph of High Street and the corner of the London Inn Square. On the right was the entrance to the Covered Arcade and the General Post Office. A horse drawn cab stands at the entrance to the London Inn Square awaiting a fare.

The Covered Arcade, a delightful construction housing numerous business premises. At a later date this scene was enhanced with floral displays. Sadly, the Arcade which was located approximately at the top of Princesshay was lost during the blitz.

Looking into the London Inn Square from High Street. The Theatre Royal is in the background.

Another view of the London Inn Square and it's centre point the New London Hotel. On the left is the Hippodrome Theatre (now Boots). A suitably attired attendant guarded the door and in a loud voice proclaimed, "early doors, pits, stalls and orchestral stalls." Numerous famous artists appeared on the stage of Hippodrome, including the great Al Jolson.

THE NEW LONDON INN

STAGE COACHES IN EXETER

The New London Inn was the centre for coaching in Exeter. Around seventy coaches a day left the New London Inn and it is estimated that around 3000 people were engaged in some way or another with coaching in the City. All mail coaches started from London, one direct, The Quicksilver was said to be the fastest in England completing the distance in around 20 hours. Coaches also left from other hotels, Half Moon, White Horse, White Lion etc. One fast coach, The Defiance did the run from London to the Clarence Hotel with a team of four greys. This often passed down Martins Lane.

On one occasion a coach piled high with Christmas Fare, hampers etc., on its way to Salisbury overturned and killed the driver. Other disasters occured, for instance when a Baron took over the reins from the driver and managed to turn over the coach. Unfortunately, the Inspector of Mail was a passenger. No unauthorised person was allowed from then on to drive the stage coaches. Naturally, horses were always at the ready, well over 100 were kept at The New London Inn and over 20 coaches passed through Heavitree alone in one day.

The New London Inn was of course one of the most important Inns in Exeter and boasted a magnificent courtyard, a photograph of which is on page 148. Among famous visitors was Robert Louis Stevenson, whose signature graced the visitors book. Also shown on the following page are plates from the commemorative dinner service for the opening of the New London Inn dated 1837. These are now in my mother's possession.

Katharine de Mattos. | S. L. Osbourne
R. L. and Mrs Stevenson | Skerryvore
Bournemouth

I cannot go without recording my obligations to everyone in the house: if it is your fate to fall sick at an inn, may heaven it may be the New London! Robert Louis Stevenson

Entry in R.L.Stevenson's Handwriting in the Visitor's Book at the New London Hotel, Exeter.

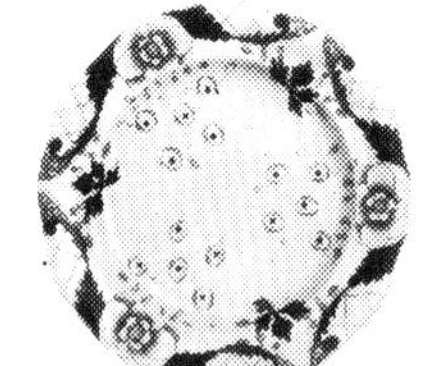
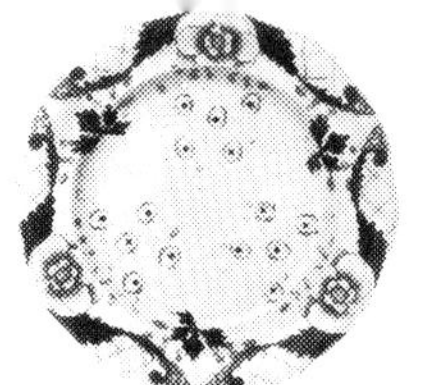
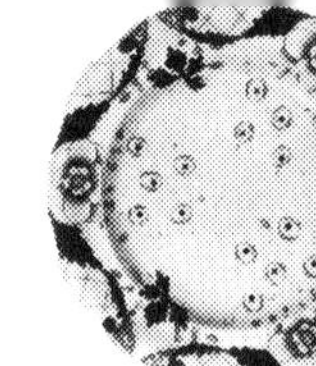

The interior of the New London Hotel, a cobbled courtyard which was covered over at a later date.

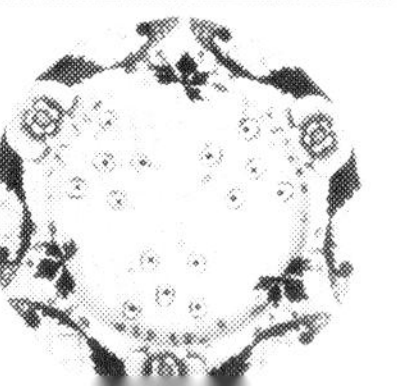

The Theatre Royal, sited neatly in the corner of the London Inn Square between Longbrook Street and New North Road.

EXETER THEATRE ROYAL

One of the most interesting buildings that existed in Exeter, the Theatre Royal had a long and fascinating history. Unfortunately, it has been one of the saddest.

The Theatre played host to some of the greatest entertainers of the stage that have been seen in this Country. The best stage shows were seen, World Premiers have opened to its floodlights. The history of this building and what it stood for would alone command a book. The site shown was the last upon which the Theatre was to stand.

Exeter's original Theatre stood in Bedford Street, but was destroyed by fire in 1820 and again in 1885. It was then transferred to the corner of Longbrook Street and New North Road.

Incredibly, even after greater fire precautions fate struck for a third time.

The romantic drama "Romany Rye" opened to a full house on September 5th 1887, a date which stands dominant in Exeter's history.

Around 10.00 p.m., a drop scene fell and was the prelude to a horrific ending to the evening. Seconds later the curtains bulged forward, not much notice was taken, once again the curtain bulged and this time someone called "Fire". A panic stricken rush took place, people fell crushing each other as they pressed to the Exit. Women jumped 40 feet from the side balcony into the street, sustaining terrible injuries.

Fire engines rushed to the scene from the Railway, Higher Barracks and Topsham. Adding to the confusion 50 horses were released from Pickfords next door and galloped off in all directions.

By the early hours of the morning the bodies were removed from the Theatre and the exact magnitude of the disaster was then realised. A horrifying total of 186 bodies were recovered. The corpses were laid out in the yard and stables of the London Inn.

At the inquest the blame was laid on bad design and construction of the building, and a lack of inspection when completed. After this, Parliament requested a complete review of the fire and safety regulations for all theatres. A result of this review was the introduction of the fire curtain and the Theatre Royal was the first to install one on rebuilding. The safety curtain would be lowered in a prompt 20 seconds. It weighed 4½ tons and took four men to winch it up.

Sadly, the Theatre Royal was demolished in 1962 and with it ended the source of some of the most interesting history of this country's Theatre. Exeter's Theatre today is no longer situated in the city centre, but housed in the University grounds. Now, an Insurance building stands on the site of the old Theatre Royal.

The aftermath of the fire showing clearly the gutted building the day after the fire. The upper and lower front balconies helped some people to escape, although many suffered severe injuries after jumping into the street below.

Inspecting the damage to the fire ravaged building.

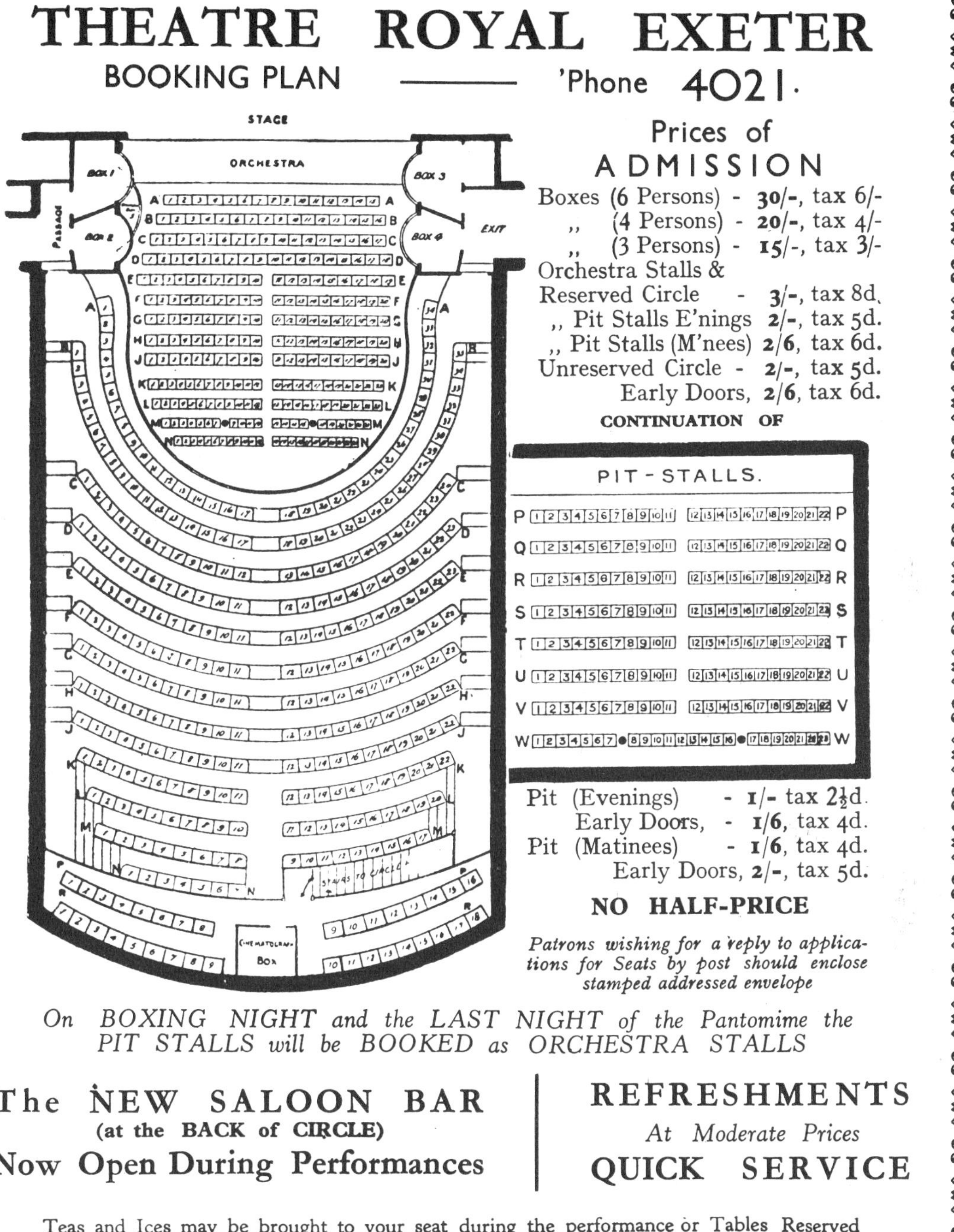

THEATRE ROYAL EXETER

BOOKING PLAN ——— 'Phone 4021.

Prices of
ADMISSION

Boxes (6 Persons) - **30/-**, tax 6/-
,, (4 Persons) - **20/-**, tax 4/-
,, (3 Persons) - **15/-**, tax 3/-
Orchestra Stalls &
Reserved Circle - **3/-**, tax 8d.
,, Pit Stalls E'nings **2/-**, tax 5d.
,, Pit Stalls (M'nees) **2/6**, tax 6d.
Unreserved Circle - **2/-**, tax 5d.
Early Doors, **2/6**, tax 6d.

CONTINUATION OF

PIT - STALLS.

Pit (Evenings) - **1/-** tax 2½d.
Early Doors, - **1/6**, tax 4d.
Pit (Matinees) - **1/6**, tax 4d.
Early Doors, **2/-**, tax 5d.

NO HALF-PRICE

Patrons wishing for a reply to applications for Seats by post should enclose stamped addressed envelope

On BOXING NIGHT and the LAST NIGHT of the Pantomime the PIT STALLS will be BOOKED as ORCHESTRA STALLS

The NEW SALOON BAR
(at the BACK of CIRCLE)
Now Open During Performances

REFRESHMENTS
At Moderate Prices
QUICK SERVICE

Teas and Ices may be brought to your seat during the performance or Tables Reserved in the Tea Room at time of booking, or may be taken in the Tea Room at the back of the Pit

BOX OFFICE OPEN 11 a.m. to 9 p.m. Phone: **Exeter 4021.**

Special Terms to Choir Parties and Schools for the Matinees on Saturdays, Jan. 2nd, Jan. 9th, Jan. 16th, Jan. 23rd, Jan. 30th, on application to Mr. Percy Dunsford, Manager.

The seating plan and prices of admission for the 1931 pantomime "Goody Two Shoes" at the Theatre Royal, Reproduced from the Pantomime Edition Programme.

OUR LITTLE GOODY TWO SHOES

FELICE LASCELLES

Felice Lascelles will make a charming Goody. Miss Lascelles had her first big part at the London Hippodrome in "Sunny," and has played under the management of, amongst others, Mr. Charles Cochran, Mr. Leslie Henson, and Mr. Jack Buchanan. One of her outstanding successes was in "Kid Boots" at the London Winter Gardens. She has a glorious wealth of wonderful hair, which shines like burnished gold, and large expressive brown eyes. She is the ideal girl for a fairy Pantomime, and she sings, acts, and dances with great grace and charm.

Felice Lascelles, who played the title role in the 1931 pantomime.

Members of Exeter Fire Brigade on a fire appliance of great antiquity, dating from 1616. Only one other example is known and that is at Windsor Castle. Date unknown.

A stroll in Northernhay Gardens. These delightful gardens situated around the ancient Castle and Moat have always been a favourite with the people of Exeter and still are today. Although the pram has changed greatly, the gardens have remained mu they were. (Circa 1900)

Paris Street. The age of the car is brought home very clearly, thanks to Maude's Motor Mart. What more could you ask for in performance, reliability and economy? A wonderful line of cars for today's collectors of vintage models.

Tram number 32, just after leaving the Tram Shed, which was later to become the bus depot.

One of Exeter's early trams.

The original horse drawn tram, pictured in Heavitree Road.

THE TRAMWAYS IN EXETER

The trams of Exeter date back to around the year 1880. For over 20 years they were horse drawn. The tracks for the trams were laid from Livery Dole to St. Davids via New North Road; Paris Street to Blackboy Road.

Great difficulties occurred with St. Davids Hill, as apparently the horses used were not of the best calibre. The problem of maintenance of road surfaces was a major factor that eventually led to the takeover by the city council, and the private company which was running the trams disolved.

The introduction of trams in Exeter caused great consternation and the public didn't respond at all well to the idea of having iron tracks placed down through High Street.

The council however, decided the trams were to become electrified. The Mayor and other notables visited a number of countries which were using trams, in order to decide the best system for Exeter.

A new generating station was built on the side of the basin to supply the trams with essential power. The new trams started in 1905.

The route for the trams was as follows:

Livery Dole to Eastgate, thence High Street, Queen Street to St. Davids. Cemetery Road to Blackboy Road and Sidwell Street to Eastgate. A route was also placed from Eastgate to Dunsford Gardens. Naturally, this route went over the new Exe Bridge. To accommodate this new track various obstructions were removed in St. Thomas.

The completed track was 4¼ miles double line 2¼ and 2¼ single line. The gauge was 3 feet 6 inches.

The system boasted 12 tram cars, which were double deckers and held 54 persons. Each car weighed 8½ tons, was 26 ft. long and was powered by two 25 horse power motors. Besides the traditional handbrake the Newall magnetic track brake was also fitted.

Costing of the Tramways

New track and wooden paving	£34000
Overhead Equipment	£ 4700
Feed Cables	£ 3000
Tramcars	£ 7000
Shed	£ 5700
Generating Plant	£ 4000
Total Cost	£58400

The mayor Mr. C. Perry drove the first tram powered by electricity, and he also drove the last in 1931.

The tram shed was then used as the bus depot until recently and demolished in 1976.

With lines being laid the tramway finally arrives in High Street. A new era was about to begin in Exeter, much to the bewildered fascination of the onlookers.

The first electrically operated tram in Exeter is driven by the Mayor, Mr. C. Perry.

Another picture of one of the first electric trams in Exeter.

The last of Exeter's trams on it's final journey driven by the Mayor, who again happened to be Mr. C. Perry.

Continuing from the London Inn Square we see a busy area in Sidwell Street. It was here that many people were engaged in catering for the stage coach service. The photograph shows horse drawn trams outside the White Lion Hotel. A fine study by the photographer.

Sidwell Street from the junction with York Road. Sidwell Street has always been a busy street and leading off it were many small courtyards and precincts, which have now disappeared. Although there has not been too great a change in the street shown in this photograph. (Circa 1912)

Upper St. Sidwell and the junction of Old Tiverton Road and Blackboy Road. In the centre is the fountain for the horses. Behind the fountain, the police box, now removed. The fountain has been resited a little further up Blackboy Road. Note the Cathedral Dairy handcart. A roundabout now stands at this junction.

The Exeter Carnival of 18th September 1907 gets off to a fine start. Raiders prepare to attack in one of the old stage coaches, while stretcher bearers stand by for casualties!

The 1911 £10,000 Daily Mail Around Britain Aeroplane Race. Take off point at the Exeter stage was Whipton playing fields.

The famous Colonel Cody prepares to leave Exeter for Salisbury on the next stage of the Around Britain Air Race on 27th July 1911. Owing to the peculiar construction of the plane it received the sobriquet of "The Cathedral".

Marking the Boundary is the Mount Pleasant Toll Gate. At this point Exeter ended and the country began. In this view we are looking down into Exeter, with the Mount Pleasant Inn directly behind the carriage. Now of course Exeter's boundaries stretch much further than they did when this photograph was taken. (Circa 1885)

CHEAP
TRAVELLING.

The only Route and Coach from Exeter, via rail to Copplestone, is the FOUR-HORSE QUEEN COACH, through Bow, Northtawton, Hatherleigh, Highampton, Holsworthy, Stratton, and Bude.

The **QUEEN FOUR-HORSE COACH** leaves SANDREY'S Falcon Hotel, Bude (*Summer and Winter*), every Monday, Wednesday, and Friday Morning, at 6-30, for Stratton, Holsworthy, Highampton, Hatherleigh, Northtawton, and Bow, to the Copplestone Station, in time for the 1-21 No. 3 Mail Train to Exeter, for the Bristol Mail and London Trains up, and for the Express and Third Class to Plymouth.

THE QUEEN COACH leaves the Copplestone Station immediately after the arrival of the 11-10 No. 3 Train from Exeter, every Tuesday, Touraday, and Saturday, and returns through the same route to the Falcon Hotel, Bude.

Every information can be obtained at SOUTHCOTT'S Bude Haven Hotel, or HUTCHINGS' Railway Hotel, Exeter, or Falcon Hotel, Bude, or Tucker's Hotel, Copplestone Station. Parcels and Goods charged at Van prices, and punctually attended to.

SANDREY, SQUIRE, & BLATCHFORD, Proprietors.

Photograph of Exeter c. 1935 by permission of Aerofilms Limited